My
Memoirs

AN AUTOBIOGRAPHY

Judge Alphonso A. Christian I

Edited by

Cora L.E. Christian, MD, MPH

PAGE PUBLISHING
Conneaut Lake, PA

First originally published by Page Publishing 2023

ISBN 978-1-6624-8465-0 (pbk)
ISBN 978-1-6624-8520-6 (hc)
ISBN 978-1-6624-8470-4 (digital)

Printed in the United States of America

CONTENTS

Foreword..v

Preface...vii

Acknowledgments ix

Chapter I: The Family I Met as a Child................................1

Chapter II: Conditions I Experienced in Saint Croix
                in Early Childhood..5

Chapter III: The Early Treatment I Received from Family.......10

Chapter IV: My Early Schooling in Frederiksted 13

Chapter V: The Bishops, Priests, and Sisters with
                Whom I Grew Up Compared with Their
                Present-Day Counterparts 18

Chapter VI: Conditions Prevailing in the Virgin
                Islands when I Graduated in the Tenth
                Grade in 1933 25

Chapter VII: How I Came to Saint Thomas to Live 29

Chapter VIII: My Three Years at the Firm of A. H.
                Lockhart & Co. Inc. 32

Chapter IX: The End of My Work at Lockhart and
                the Experience I Had Immediately Thereafter......36

Chapter X: My Three Years after I Left the Firm of
                A. H. Lockhart & Co.: 1937 to 1940 41

Chapter XI: My Entrance into Politics as a Member of
                the Progressive Guide and My Experience
                Therein, Especially with Several
                Members of the Legislature, Including a
                Majority and a Minority Bloc 46

Chapter XII: My Study of Law and My Admission to
                  the Bar after Two Tries: One Unofficial
                  and One Official..52
Chapter XIII: My Family Life 60
Chapter XIV: The Housing Situation in the Islands and
                  How It Forced Me to Struggle to Own
                  My Own Home..66
Chapter XV: Why I Wished so Hard to Give My
                  Children the Best Education Possible................74
Chapter XVI: My Experiences in Public Life..........................80
Chapter XVII: My Periods of Intense Agony in the
                  Practice of the Law 90
Chapter XVIII: The Creation of the Office of Senior
                  Sitting Judge of the Territorial Court 105
Chapter XIX: A Final Perspective...109
Chapter XX: Conclusion 113
Book Review of My Memoirs: An Autobiography 117

Alphonso A. Christian I

This work is intended to be an autobiography. I hope it will serve as an encouragement and an inspiration to not only members of my family, which is quite large, but also to all Virgin Islanders of all races and classes to always have and nurture the faith and hope that—by perseverance, never accepting no or discouragement for an answer—they can succeed.

This book will trace my most humble beginnings as a barefoot boy from a deeply Roman Catholic religious family through my early childhood and education in Saint Croix, my transfer to Saint Thomas, and my social, educational, political, and professional experiences in Saint Thomas and in the Virgin Islands as a whole.

I dedicate this book to my maternal grandparents, Theresa and Alexander Benjamin; my parents, Wilhelmena and Peter Christian; my immediate family, Ruth and the children; and my community of all Virgin Islanders. But I dedicate it principally to my last child, Cora L.E. Christian, MD, MPH, who literally sat on me, drove me on until I put pen to paper, began, and completed this task. Her efforts in this direction are another illustration of the value of the virtue that a great cleric (Archbishop Fulton J. Sheen) said at the commencement exercises of my nephew-in-law (Dr. Alfred O. Heath) in 1957 is the greatest of all the virtues—perseverance. Without that on her part and mine, this undertaking would not have materialized.

PREFACE

Cora L. E. Christian, MD, MPH

Why did I push my dad to write his autobiography? It is because covering the period 1916–1991, we will all clearly discover an awareness of our distinctive cultural heritage through the life of one who indeed found an opening behind every wall and challenge placed in front of him. Alphonso A. Christian I's conviction that a real human revolution occurs when one has a good relationship with oneself, one's immediate family, one's work environment whether subordinate or supervisor, the public, and one's Creator. To the generations of Virgin Islanders restlessly searching for purpose and identity, he gives a telling narrative of significant events, personalities, attitudes of a mostly unrecorded past, as well as the atmosphere under which a person with his characteristics achieved. You can judge for yourself whether his conclusion that destiny is not a matter of chance. It is a matter of choice. It is not a thing to be waited for. It is a thing to be achieved.

ACKNOWLEDGMENTS

My most profound appreciation to all who interacted with my dad throughout his life. Each of you contributed to shaping who he was, whether in a leap of faith in believing in him or the obstacles you put in his path. A special thanks to the reviewers who took their expertise in politics, the law, and history to read these memoirs and share their thoughts about the importance of his journey of almost ninety years before his passing. And finally, to my family members—especially my husband, Simon; my daughter, Nesha; and son, Marcus—who confirmed to me that it was essential to have these memoirs published for too often we do not have the opportunity to know our ancestors in the details that my dad shared in his memoirs.

CHAPTER I

The Family I Met as a Child

Willhelmena Benjamin Christian, Mother

I was born in Frederiksted, Saint Croix, at Number Forty Prince Street to Peter and Wilhelmena Christian, on August 2, 1916. I was the tenth child in a family of fifteen (15) children. My mother informed me that, as I was born on August 2nd—the feast of Saint Alphonsus Ligouri—the Belgian priest who baptized me gave me the name Alphonsus. This is precisely how it appears on my baptismal record. I ended up with both Alphonsus and Augustine, the latter probably taken from the name of the month in which I was born.

It appears that in those days, there were several strong factors relating to naming children, which are not quite so evident in our time. First, most families appeared to be very close to the church. The parents did not place as much emphasis on naming their children as people do today. They may have been too busy trying to eke out a bare livelihood. Thirdly, they seem to have been quite content

1

to let their parish priest provide a suitable name. Invariably, he would select a suitable Saint name for the child. This is especially true in Saint Croix, where the Roman Catholic Church was most influential.

Peter Christian, Father

As a young boy, in addition to my father, mother, brothers, and sisters, I was very close to my maternal grandparents, especially my grandfather, Alexander Benjamin—who, next to my parents and teachers, exerted a most powerful influence on my life and character formation. My mother was the embodiment of womanly virtue, the true heart of the home, in spite of rather harsh treatment received at the hands and from the tongue of my father. From my father, I believe I inherited most of my innate ability and drive to learn and the desire to pursue and acquire knowledge with some appreciable degree of success. And from the stability of the union of my father and mother—as volatile as it was, lasting as it did for fifty-four (54) years until death, the death of my father—I obtained my appreciation of the value of a stable home.

But it was from Alexander Benjamin that I had inculcated in me many of the viewpoints, concepts, and perspectives, which were to support and carry me through, especially in difficult times in the future. True, I was conditioned by my father to survive and endure under great strain and pressure. For instance, our work period began from the time we were five years of age and ran from five in the morning to midnight—if necessary, for seven days a week in all kinds of weather and included both hard physical and mental work in and out of the classroom.

But Grandfather inculcated in my thoughts like the following:

Always endeavor not only to get a good education but also solid economic security. These are mutually and reciprocally supportive and protective. One without the other could be woefully inadequate.

Be careful not to be property rich and money poor or vice versa. Here again, a partnership works best.

It is not the color of the Buckra (the White man) that people adore and that they Mister all the time but his resources. If you equal him in the acquisition and possession of those materials, educational, moral, and spiritual resources, the difference of color would more often than not be artificial and inconsequential.

Never spend all you earn. The first thing you do with every paycheck is put away a part for the future and never touch your savings, except in the most dire circumstances. And don't claim that you are not earning enough. It could have been nothing.

If you want something, go for it. If you don't want it, send for it.

Never covet another man's goods, especially another man's wife. This is the greatest sin of all and could be the most dangerous and disastrous, according to the old man.

It is better to die and leave than to live and want.

Finally, when in the doldrums, remember the best moment of your life is the one you are living now. Treat it as such and your whole perspective, attitude, and feeling will change for the better.

It is only as I grew up and tried to apply these tenets that I began to appreciate their real worth. That is why I dedicated this work to my parents and grandparents for putting together the principles of life, the guidelines they taught me, and applying these in my day-to-day life as best I could. It has not always been easy, as you could well imagine, particularly with respect to some of these principles. But because of my observance of them, I have been able to weather some rather stormy experiences, as it were, to come through many a crucible the stronger for having been so victimized.

When my maternal grandfather passed on at age ninety-four (94), my father at age seventy-nine (79), and my mother at age eighty-seven (87), they had indeed (for good or ill) passed on to me and to my brothers and sisters a great body of living aids, which (if properly applied) could not only help but be most beneficial to us.

The parish in whose choir my father was a chief tenor for forty (40) years, Saint Patrick's in Frederiksted, paid him due honor at his funeral rites. They turned out en masse in a procession led by the then pastor, Father Arthur Donnelly (pastor, 1956–1959), and the community band with several hundred other relatives, friends, and acquaintances, proceeding from the old hospital through the streets of Frederiksted to the church to honor Peter Christian. It was for me a most moving and comforting experience.

When my mother passed on, she received the singular honor of having seven priests led by our beloved bishop, His Excellency Edward J. Harper, conduct a most comforting, impressive, and dignified funeral service for her. I was deeply touched. These ministers of the church went all out to honor our dear mother, and I wrote Bishop Harper, expressing to them my deep appreciation for the beautiful final tribute they paid Wilhelmena Christian.

As I was living in Saint Thomas at the time of his death, I was not privileged to attend the funeral of the grand old man, Alexander Benjamin. But I was informed that he received a most suitable burial by the church attested to by the presence of many of his townspeople.

CHAPTER II

Conditions I Experienced in Saint Croix in Early Childhood

Needless to say, conditions prevailing in Saint Croix when I was a young boy were vastly different from those at present. Indeed, they were so different that some examples may well startle the reader. Surely, for the benefit of history and the contemporary generation, what we had to contend with and make do with in those days should be recorded.

To provide some perspective of time, I am writing of the time from 1920 to about 1936. These were the early days of American sovereignty over the Islands. But the Danish ways were still much in evidence many years after the changed sovereignty, which occurred March 31, 1917.

Politically, all but a very limited few, about 99 percent of the population, were disenfranchised. Unless you had a certain minimum amount of property and annual income, you could not exercise that wellspring, fountainhead, of citizenship—the right to vote. And without that voice in who represented you and made the laws that governed you, you just did not count.

This deprivation of the rights, privileges, and power of citizenship—the power of the vote—spilled over to deprive one of his unalienable right to life, liberty, and the pursuit of happiness. Strong words? Yes but so true. If you could not say who would make your laws and generally represent you in government, you had no say in who your legislators, governor, or judges would be either. To be accused of a crime is almost to be convicted of that crime, for you had no voice in the operation of your government—whether the legislative, executive, or judicial; mediately or immediately; and indirectly or directly. If bad laws were made, you had no say in changing them. You dared not disagree with the Executive, for you had no real civil power to speak to him and command his respect. Justice for the burgher and his son was something quite different from justice for the disenfranchised and his son.

A good friend of mine, the late Arnold LaFontaine, in or about 1965 gave me an illustration of the truth of this crass inequality under law—of government of men and not of laws, if you will. He told me how my good friend and legal mentor, the late beloved Judge C. G. Thiele—the last remnant of Danish officialdom in the Islands, whom I later succeeded as Police Judge—dealt with some men found gambling in the building owned by a tenant of mine, Mr. Cecil Allen. Here were six young men, three the offspring of the landed gentry and three the children of the so-called hoi polloi. Found in the act, they were all arrested or invited to appear at the police station. Taken into the judge's chambers, Mr. LaFontaine told me that the three privileged youth were severely scolded by the judge for being found gambling with such as the other three, while the latter were sentenced to spend some time, albeit slight, in Fort Christian.

I relate this story not to reflect in any degree badly on the judge. He was only enforcing the prevailing will or custom of the society or more accurately, of the ruling class of that day. After all, they were paying him to do just that very job. And he had taken an oath of office to abide by the laws and mores and customs of the people of that day, who (for all practical purposes) were the ruling class (the land barons), who were also the politically endowed, the voters, and the power structure.

It does not take much imagination either to see that political power led to economic power. The children of the enfranchised owned almost all the land, almost all the businesses, and surely, all the respected public offices. They even had the best seats reserved for them in the churches. The disenfranchised got what they did not want.

And inevitably, these political, economic, and resulting social privileges and perquisites led to better educational opportunities for the privileged, which were sometimes taken advantage of, sometimes not. But the important fact is that they were there for the asking at the feet of the privileged but were studiously and vigorously denied to the disenfranchised. Indeed, the enfranchised did all they could to prevent the creation of even a free public high school in the Islands.

True, sometimes the ease of obtaining these benefits led to their being so little appreciated that—as we shall see later—quite often, the siblings of this privileged class grew up to be the underprivileged educationally, while the erstwhile underprivileged and disadvantaged yearned so avidly and worked so assiduously to acquire a good education that following the advent of universal suffrage by virtue of the passage of the Organic Act of 1936, there resulted a virtual turning of the tables in this respect. Some may say that what we are seeing is retribution, the sins of the parents falling on the children. But I, for one, am not wise enough to provide the answer to this most perplexing question. Suffice it to say that this subject is the source of considerable puzzlement, frustration, and suffering among the afflicted, the once very specially privileged class of society.

But it was not only in the political, economic, and educational realms that the difference was great. The streets and roads were all of rocks and dust when dry and rocks and mud when it rained. There was no electricity in any public place and in very few homes. Thus at night, apart from a very few and far between gas lamps, the Islands were pitch dark.

Nevertheless, crimes were not rampant in those days, for we had a closed society, isolated and insulated from the rest of the world. And the discipline of adults and the legal authorities was stern and on children, even sterner.

As for the availability of water, we had only a few public and private wells—a cistern here and there, usually in the center of the yard taking up what today would be regarded as precious space and the big sea, without desalination plants, working or not working.

There was obviously no TV, no radio, no Wi-fi, no motion pictures, and no automobiles for the most part. These and other conveniences came one by one later, in some cases, much later.

Before I leave this chapter, I must say a further word about the discipline of youth in this period in the Virgin Islands. Unlike today, every adult was a kind of parens patriae. This is a term used by the law, which means father or parent of the whole country as distinguished from parent of just one child or private family. So as such parent of the whole assembly or community of children, each adult took a deep and abiding interest in the proper behavior and upbringing of every child whether of his own blood or household or not. If an adult saw any child do any improper act, that adult could discipline that child; yes, even apply corporal punishment to that child as in the best judgment of that adult the circumstances reasonably warranted and that was the end of the matter. At least, the child desperately hoped it was the end of the matter, for if the incident reached the ears of the parent or guardian of that child, woe betide, for the child would almost certainly be disciplined even more severely by its own household also.

Today, which adult would dare discipline a child not his own? If words were used, he would be victim to a barrage of verbal abuse, first from the child and then probably from its household also. And if he were insane enough to touch that child, the parents or guardians would very probably haul him into court—both on the criminal and on the civil side as well—and try their utmost to subject him to criminal fines, jail, and the payment of civil damages.

And this is not limited to persons who are strangers to the child, who are not in loco parentis, but applies to even teachers, relatives, or friends. Add this basic, far-reaching change in our customs and mores to instant knowledge of crimes, the how and when as they are committed in all parts of the world by the media of radio and TV; the visual, graphic portrayals of the movies and television; the greater knowledge of the law of crimes acquired from wider and greater readership abilities; the desecration and disintegration of the family and home; and the vast increase in materialism and secularism of the world. And you must perforce ask yourself if there is any reasonable wonder left as to why the youth have degenerated into the social jungle that plagues us today.

We, *Homo sapiens*, the adults, not the youth, have sown that wind. And we, the adults, have reaped a whirlwind. For instance, statistics show that at least 50 percent of men who father children either abandon them completely or have to be continually forced to assume their just responsibility of supporting, raising, and training their offspring. Even the animals are superior in this respect. The birds build a nest, a house, for their young before they court, lay eggs, and bring them forth. Indeed, every species of animals I know provides for its young better than man, the species made in the image and likeness of the Great Creator. I have always admired the people of French descent here (at least those of the older generation) for this practice of providing (if it be only a little coop) to shelter their young before bringing them forth. Yes, I would ask it, not rhetorically but directly and forthrightly: Are we not guilty of contributing substantially to the degeneration of our people? Do we not have a lot to learn from even the animals in this respect?

There was a time when we were forbidden from having a typical Christian family. It was thought to be too good, too dignified, for us. Now we have that opportunity. I ask that the reader cherish it, use it, preserve it, and be patient with it to the end. With all its difficulties, it is far superior to any other relationship for the security and happiness of its principals, the proper raising of children, and the efficacious and beneficial perpetuation and enjoyment of the human race.

CHAPTER III

The Early Treatment I Received from Family

As I grew up, I learned very quickly (even before I reached the proverbial age of reason) that my father was very demanding—strict to the point of being severe as to the observance of acceptable standards of behavior, hardworking, and very religious in the Roman Catholic mold of the day.

We have already laid out the almost-complete absence of living comforts, which are taken for granted today that marked the quality of life of the early 1900s. I would add only that we used discarded clothes affectionately called lodging in the place of a mattress, boxes, and pieces of board called laths as a bedstead and spring. And three to four boys slept in one room, the only other furnishing of which were a few simple chairs or boxes, religious pictures, and mail order catalog pages as decorations for the walls of our room. And the room was the junk heap for anything for which storage space could not be found elsewhere, including most of the literally hundreds of carpenter's tools of my father who was, at the time, a top-notch carpenter generally known as Boss Pete.

Because my parents operated large tracts of farmland for the raising and cultivation of sugarcane and table edibles of all kinds—including ground provisions, vegetables, and native fruits—one area to which our strict mode of life did not extend was that of the availability of food. There was always an overabundance, a veritable plenitude of that, to the point where we had to work diligently to keep spoilage to a minimum. This constant presence of food always tempted me to conclude that for all the many difficult conditions of life, which our parents, particularly our father, imposed on us, God must have endowed us with at least this partial benediction on our lifestyle as a quid pro quo of sorts—a true source of comfort and consolation.

That lifestyle was no picnic. As soon as we could reason, our day started at 5:00 a.m. and continued until the work of a family of two parents and many children to take care of—who operated a large farm with many horses, mules, donkeys, hogs, chickens, and a large carpenter practice—was complete at night. And this could go to 1:00 a.m.

That work included the following: tending the animals; collecting feed for them; cleaning the house, yard, and stables; assisting in planting, cultivating, cleaning, and reaping the ground produce; marketing the ground produce with the aid of baskets or trays; cooking and cleaning for the family; attending school; and strictly observing of the church laws. In many cases, there was pouring rain when we awoke, but the show had to go on. On a typical day after feeding the animals, we would have to harness them and go out to gather feed for one or more days; return; unharness and secure the animals; clean up to attend school; eat during the lunch hour; rush out and sell what we could of the farm produce, which might otherwise spoil; rush back and attend school during the afternoon; after school, rush back and either proceed to do some more selling, housekeeping work, or proceed to the farm to cultivate, plant, weed, reap more produce and fruits for sale; drive back from the country to our town house; and unharness and secure the animals, the cart, and the farm products.

After that, we would eat, do our school homework, and await the arrival home of our father in his spring cart or buggy to unharness and secure his horse and cart and its contents for the evening.

I am told that the first three of the eight children who lived to grow up broke under this strain and ran away. My brother, Peter, was the first to stay, followed by me and the three that followed me, the last of whom is Ann Christian Abramson—who, among other distinctions, became the first native woman to be elected to the local legislature.

I have to say a word about my brother, Peter, being the first to make it. Sure, I must admit he deserves considerable credit. But I suspect that being named after the old man, the fact that the old man had begun to lose some of his earlier vigor, truculence, and unremitting severity, and the fact that times were favorable to a more enlightened view—all these factors may well have jointly contributed to that most propitious and welcome result.

There is an irony that always tempers my strong earlier impatience and dissatisfaction with the lifestyle imposed on the entire family by our father. Notwithstanding that apparent or ostensible terrible situation, all the five children did remarkably well in their studies at school—in many cases, topping the entire class. All things do seem to work well for those who believe in the Lord. At least that was how my father rationalized the end result of a lifestyle, which was imposed on the children and which was, to me, at least at the time, intolerable. This is one fact I would admit, though: It seemed to have been providential (in that it prepared and conditioned me) to survive with a remarkable degree of stoicism and composure many rigid and awesome tests, which were to be visited on me in later life, and notwithstanding these (or perhaps even because of them) to achieve positively beyond my wildest dreams.

CHAPTER IV
———————

My Early Schooling in Frederiksted

My schooling began in Saint Patrick's Parochial School at age six. Whether it was in kindergarten or first grade, I cannot recall, but I know there were 105 in the class. And when I graduated in the tenth grade, there were only about fifteen (15) left. The inexorable selective process had taken its grim toll. So heavy dropout rates are nothing new in this Territory.

I was particularly grateful to God, my parents, and my teachers for two factors. The first was I had made it to the top of the class in spite of what I considered intolerable social, cultural, and economic factors. Notwithstanding the hard daily discipline of our family life, our strict adherence to our Catholic faith, and the plenitude of all kinds of self-grown food, provisions and vegetables no doubt were redeeming, counterbalancing factors. I was too young and immature to put things in their proper perspective; to separate the fundamentals of a meaningful life from the superficial, such as an overabundance of time to play and even idle; to dress in the most modern attire; to look the acceptable best in color and racial appearance; and to pal around with the girls.

Secondly, for the first time in the history of Saint Patrick's, graduation exercises would be held in the church. This was in June 1933, and the valedictorian did not have to give an address. How I dreaded having to do that at the time!

But Father Edward Baumann, who at the time was pastor and addressed as Father Superior, as all Roman Catholic priests who were pastors were addressed at the time, more than made up for the new beginning and what would no doubt have been less than an amateurish job on my part. I have never forgotten his theme: I have fought the good fight. I have finished the course. I have kept the faith. Saint Paul must have applauded in heaven as we drank in, enjoyed, and were richly edified by his beautiful composition and delivery.

But back to the early years of schooling. I have already detailed all the things all the Christian children had to do while going to school. I had a particularly hard time because I was Alphonso, who immediately followed my brother Peter, who—in addition to being named after my father for which he enjoyed some degree of extra love and favoritism—was much stronger physically than I was and therefore, more suited to standing up well (even admirably) under the great load of work and study that was required of us for seven days a week and twelve (12) to sixteen (16) hours a day. Besides, I was born myopic and never was given the privilege of receiving eyeglasses until after I graduated from school. Needless to say, this did not help my productivity, especially with regard to the more laborious work for which my brothers and sisters will recall I was never well suited. In fact, compared to Peter (I would describe him as robust, sinewy, and strong), I was half blind and frail, quite unsuited to hard physical labor.

Yet in spite of all the above, I had to bear my fair share of the work or I would receive my fair share of verbal and corporal chastisement—to put it in present-day terms and to put it mildly.

For my teachers—those beautiful, pioneering, highly exemplary Belgian sisters, especially Mother Ermine, Mother Leona, and Mother Xaveria (she was very classy and beautiful but severe)—I have the highest praise. There are innumerable incidents indelibly etched in the recesses of my mind and in my heart that to me were proof conclusive of the ability, understanding, compassion, and piety of these fine servants of God in what then was a most uncomfortable, backward, and most underdeveloped corner of the world.

As soon as these Sisters discovered I could not see far, they placed me right up in the front of the class, where I could read the blackboard fairly easily. This probably had the spinoff benefit of their being able to keep better tabs on me and that in turn, probably acted as an added factor in making me more attentive and productive in the class. I remember well when we received one of our first lessons in biology. I just barely smiled when I saw a human skeleton presented to the class. That smile was quickly visible to Mother Xaveria, only a few feet from me. "Don't you ever smile when these lessons are being given. This is not a fun thing but one of science" was her strong and firm admonition. And as those who knew Mother Xaveria well will tell you when she gave an order, you complied always.

Another incident in this connection, which sticks out in my mind, is one, which occurred when I was in the fifth grade. I had been very sick for about six weeks and therefore, had not been able to attend classes before the last lessons before an examination preparatory to card time or to take the exam. Yet the sister rated me as first in the class. This understandably caused a furor, or at least a good deal of murmuring in the class. This was the teacher's explanation, "He has proved that had he been here, he would be the first in the class. His absence is none of his doing and is only temporary." And for the time being, at least, the protest ended. But I realized that it now devolved upon me to justify and vindicate as conclusively as I could that lavish expression of faith in me by that Sister, and this I tried to do on my recovery and return to the class.

There was another reason for my hard work at this time. The constant breather down my back was that venerable lady, Helen Joseph Williams—brilliant daughter of newspaper editor and publisher of the *West End News*, Paul Joseph, who almost overtook me. But in those days, male chauvinism was somewhat stronger than it is today, and I guess I had my fair share of it. I must admit that unlovely quality is what may have kept me going when the course was roughest.

Diploma from St. Patrick's Parochial School, June 25, 1933

Graduating in the flood tide of the great depression was at once harmful and beneficial. Those were the NRA, WPA, CCC days. There was no work, particularly for a social parvenu like me, who was just a fairly good beginning stenographer, bookkeeper, and typist. I say a parvenu because I did not belong to the racial, color, or social class to whom this type of work was given. In fact, to this class, I was a complete pariah, absolutely misplaced and despised—being the son of Mr. and Mrs. Peter Christian (a solid grass-roots family, who graduated as head of his commercial class, with some very favorable publicity from the *West End News*, the church commencement service, and the school play, and who was prepared to work in stenography, which was an art in very short supply at the time). All these factors counted for little, favoring as they did the wrong person.

So I ended up as a $1-a-day typist in an NRA office at Estate Anna's Hope, Saint Croix. This was perhaps providential because I quickly got the reputation of being the fastest typist on the floor, and this would help me later to qualify to be sent to Saint Thomas in the second important post of my career, which I will deal with later.

However, before I sought work, almost immediately on my graduation, the priests and sisters counseled with my parents as to what to do with me next. The priests and sisters were determined that I should continue my education and become a priest. That was quickly squelched by my father who reasoned that they were not going to tuck me away in some faraway, hidden corner of Africa. "After all," he said, "all priests in the Western world were White or looked White." But when the alternative professions of law and medicine were mentioned, he countered with what now appears to be quite an inane argument, although it was true then that there were thousands of these professionals walking the streets of the States hungry and so I should not join their ranks. I say inane, for obviously that rather wise old man must have at least suspected that the depression, as great and pervasive as it was, would not last forever.

Now I only believe I know why he acted as he did. It was the long-established custom in those days that the descendants of the slaves should not get an education beyond their thirteenth (13th) year, if indeed they should get that much. Remember, I am talking about life in the twenties and early thirties of the twentieth century. You surely remember the fight that took place as late as the early thirties to establish a public, accredited high school. Now I had violated that rule by going to school until sixteen (16). I was superannuated by three long years, and tradition and the mores of the time—and especially my father—were waiting with bated breath for me to go to work and repay my parents and society for all they had done for me up to such an old age. How then could the priests, the sisters, and I, or anyone else have the temerity to suppose that I should continue my education after age sixteen (16)? Thus, the answer of the old man was a peremptory no.

CHAPTER V
_____

The Bishops, Priests, and Sisters with Whom I Grew Up Compared with Their Present-Day Counterparts

There are some significant differences of form, if not of substance, in the lifestyles of the clergy and the nuns of my early childhood as compared with their counterparts of today. Manifestly, it is not as simple a task as might be first imagined to draw a line of demarcation here, which is both realistic and of some clear value.

But a perspective should help achieve these two desirable ends. The bishop, priests, and sisters of that day were ministering to a completely different class of people—educationally, economically, socially, and especially politically. They were dealing with a comparatively much smaller community of people—who, for the most part, were only one or two generations removed from an ancestry, which had suffered the dehumanization, degradation, and stenches of slavery for centuries. These people were very poor, largely uneducated, politically disenfranchised, and impotent—a people almost totally despised, oppressed, and without meaningful rights or privilege.

By contrast, notwithstanding all their present weaknesses, the people presently ministered to by the clergy and religious of today are several generations removed from the stenches and curse of slavery. They enjoy the highest standard of living of all the peoples of the

Caribbean. They enjoy the opportunities of a high school and college education for those able and willing to avail themselves of these advantages for self-improvement. They enjoy the means of inspiration and motivation afforded by seeing their own hold and ably acquit themselves in discharging the duties of the highest offices and professions in their home in and out of government. They are not only enfranchised but hold considerable political power. And they are beginning to show signs of moving from the socially and culturally disadvantaged and deprived into the appreciation and enjoyment of some of the richer indicia and refinements of an affluent society.

To state at this point that it was much easier to minister to the not-so-privileged ancestors of today's population than the task of the present ministers of the gospel is a much more difficult and complex one is obviously an understatement. I would say that compared to the people of the Virgin Islands of today, their ancestors were little more than an Amen people. Indeed, it is not uncommon for bishops, priests, and sisters of today to openly acknowledge the fact that many of their congregation are much more educated, informed than they. And when they say this, they are not referring to special bodies of learning or disciplines or specialized professions but to education in general.

I earnestly trust I shall not be considered as insensitive when I say this hard fact of life must come as quite a traumatic shock to many of these servants of the servants of God. Due to the enormous overall difference in the general class of the people they serve, no more is the clergy the educational elite of society. No more is their word taken as the law. No more can they equate what they want with what God wants of you. No more can they just get up at masses and services unprepared and ramble on or deliver the same routine pious sermons or homilies with few, if any, of their parishioners and followers being the wiser or treating the squandering of their time with indifference. Pardon the characterization in this connection if you are inclined to think it impious, but the religious ministers of today are in an entirely new ball game.

I sometimes wonder what substantial effects the changes outlined in this aspect of our life, the ministry of our spiritual life in these Islands, have had in several areas. Has the growing magnitude of the job caused a falling-off of entrants into religious vocations? Has it shocked some who began prior to its full impact into discontinuing before completion of their initial qualifying studies to be priests and nuns? Could the magnitude of this change in fitness for a workmanlike job in contemporary society have shocked some who were already in the institution and serving according to their binding vows to leave and seek less onerous occupations? How comfortable, happy, and content are the unfit—the deadwood—that remain? What increased erosion of this commitment has inevitably resulted from the increased materialism and secularism of contemporary society? As each reader of this takes the time to make a close and studied observation, he may get true answers.

To return to the perspective, I remember my maternal grandfather's attitude toward the church. First, the only true church was the One, Holy, (Roman) Catholic and Apostolic Church. What the priest (not necessarily the Pope or bishop) said (and if the Pope, not necessarily ex cathedra, or on matters of faith and morals) was law. It was wrong to end the Our Father with For Thine is the Kingdom and the Power and the Glory, etc. Although ironically, the Roman Church is now using those same words in its liturgy while Dean Thomas W. Gibbs III of the Anglican Church vindicates my grandfather by saying he was right. Also, entering any but a Catholic Church building for worship was a mortal sin.

I remember changing my strict adherence to that last tenet only when I began working in politics in the Virgin Islands Progressive Guide in 1938. At that time, there was no TV and little of either radio or the press that one could use to build up a viable political base. You had to meet and greet, press flesh and exchange and dialogue, with the people to build up your constituency where you could find them. And one place you could find the people quite often was in the churches.

To the founders of the Virgin Islands Progressive Guide— Carlos Downing, Omar Brown, and Henry V. Richards Jr.—and an early hard worker of that organization, the late Valdemar A. Hill, necessity was the mother of invention and this political invention did the job. Whenever we could, we met and addressed the people in their churches. Yet I had my qualms of conscience, my scruples. But viewed in the light of what our church is advocating today so that we may heed Christ's injunction to become one (flock), the exchange of pulpits by Catholic and Protestant ministers every year, their urging of their Catholic parishioners to attend services in all Protestant churches—ecumenism, you know—it now appears that my early scruples were quite unnecessary. But we must admit that these crass changes (inconsistencies, indeed complete about-faces), even in the name of that euphemism (ecumenism), tend to create skeptics, cynics, and agnostics (if not outright atheists) and worse, to erode the membership, the parishioners, of the Catholic church.

My father was perhaps not as fanatic and bigoted a Catholic as my grandfather. I remember Father Carlisle Blake (our first native pastor at Saints Peter and Paul) on Sunday, May 8, 1977, while preaching most eloquently as he always does on Mother's Day—describing Saint Peter as our greatest saint. That reminded me of my father, Peter Christian Sr.—God rest him. He always felt he had the name of the greatest of saints. He also loved the church dearly. This love, no doubt, inspired and motivated him to also love all its ministers, especially the bishops and pastors; to be virtually awed by their carriage, vestments, and ministries; to give them the first and choicest fruits of his farm; to contribute the best of his great skill as a carpenter in the building, maintenance, and improvement of the church, presbytery, and other church buildings; and most importantly, to serve as chief tenor in the choir of Saint Patrick's in Frederiksted, which he did for forty (40) years.

Many of the children of my parents still love and serve the church with a steady and remarkable zeal. And probably nothing will change them. But what of their children, the true contemporary generation, on whom the pillars of society must rely for its continued life and health? Suffice it to say that although all my children enjoyed good careers (both scholastic and religious) in Saints Peter and Paul High School and in Catholic undergraduate colleges—Santa Maria in Ponce, Notre Dame in South Bend, and Marquette in Wisconsin—there is where their participation and loyalty come to a screeching halt. In fact, there was not only a halt but a complete change of heart and spirit, an antagonism instead of love and appreciation. In one case, there was even an apostasy. I can only hope this is temporary, notwithstanding the fact that it is so widespread among this general class, the adolescents, high school graduates, and generally the young adults of today.

Some day, they might realize that had the Belgian and American priests and sisters who originally began their religious mission work in the Islands not come here, I might not have received even that modest beginning I enjoyed. And had I not received even that modest beginning, I might not have been able to develop to the point where I was able to give them a more impressive preparation for their life's work in which they take so much pride and which serves them so well today.

Another difference that seems to have gained weight and currency relates to the matters of commitment and hard work in the spirit of the vows of chastity, poverty, and obedience. Some people wonder if these vows are still made. And if so, do they mean anything? Wittingly or unwittingly, many new changes in the lifestyles of particularly the nuns have completely scandalized much of the laity and the public in general and severely hurt the church.

The complete conviction that the lifestyles of the religious of an earlier era created in the laity the belief that the church and its ministers constituted something sacred, an ideal to be looked up to, priests you could respect and prostrate yourself before in sorrow and confess your sins as you would to Christ Himself—that conviction and its concomitant respect are all but destroyed and lost. And ironically, this wreckage was done and is being done assiduously and quite insouciantly, although perhaps by sheer inadvertence, by the very people who should preserve and guard it diligently as sacred and inviolate, if for no other reason since the continuation of their time-honored vocation—even their livelihood—depends upon these important ingredients.

This is not to say that the religious among us are not doing great work. I am only pointing out the fact that just maybe they are not giving sufficient thought, attention, and effort to preserving the great respect in which they and their professions have been traditionally held in the Caribbean in the past.

But our hope is that the Holy Spirit has something to do with all this. And as the Chief Architect has promised, the Church will overcome, continue, endure, and even grow—hopefully strong in spite of it all.

I would be somewhat remiss if I did not record in this chapter the beginning, growth, and administration of the Catholic Diocese of Saint Thomas in the Virgin Islands.

This new institution in Catholicism in the United States Virgin Islands began in 1960 with the creation of the Prelature of the Virgin Islands with the Most Reverend Bishop Edward J. Harper, appointed and installed as the first incumbent head or prelate. This beginning in all its constituent parts has since its first moment to the present been one of the great plusses and blessings of the church in these Islands. It came at a most propitious time to guide the faithful through the turbulent waters of the new ecumenism, which was to suddenly confront Catholicism and all the rest of Christendom. This new effort might very well have been a blessing, but we all know too well the inevitable problems one has in adapting mankind quite suddenly to big, bold new concepts. The establishment of aggiornamento in Roman Catholicism was no exception.

Surely, the approval and use of this new church policy has had its plusses, but its minuses just cannot be overlooked or minimized. Perhaps its greatest minus is its potential for eroding the strength of the Catholic faithful even more than the extent or proportion to which it unifies the Christian denominations, which was perhaps its stated primary objective.

But the one factor that contributed mightily to the growth of the prelature was the incumbency of Bishop Harper, our first resident bishop. His many personal gifts—an exceptionally pleasing personality, innate ability, excellent training, and adaptability to tireless service in and out of the church to mention just a few—all served to pilot the new institution in Roman Catholicism in a relatively new and most volatile era with an abundance of wisdom and good discretion so that when the church was mentioned, both it and the

Bishop, were richly loved and respected by all people of all faiths and persuasions in all the United States and the British Virgin Islands.

After twenty (20) years of the Bishop's able guidance of the prelature, the powers that be were satisfied that the prelature was indeed ready to be advanced to a full diocese. And so it was in 1980, with the investiture of Bishop Harper as its first Bishop, that the Diocese of Saint Thomas in the Virgin Islands was created. Now in its second year, as we write these Memoirs, the wise and discreet administration of the Bishop continues to guide, build, and preserve the church.

I have no doubt that all who read these lines will join in solemn prayer that the Bishop will enjoy good health and strength to continue to serve as ably and well until he attains his seventy-fifth (75th) year when retirement is mandatory—that after retirement, he will remain among us until the inevitable end and that God will then bless the Roman Catholic Diocese in the Virgin Islands with a successor who will adapt himself to his office as well and love and serve the people of his Diocese as much as His Excellency Bishop Edward J. Harper.

I consider it an honor and great source of pride to be able to say that I have personally served on the Bishop's Diocesan Advisory Board, have been his legal advisor for many years, and that he was not only my Bishop but my personal friend almost from the beginning of his episcopal ministry in the Virgin Islands. I say without hesitation that here was a true spiritual leader who served as if he was really and truly called and was not just sent or did not just go into the priestly or religious ministry of the church.

CHAPTER VI

Conditions Prevailing in the Virgin Islands when I Graduated in the Tenth Grade in 1933

I graduated in June 1933 from Saint Patrick's School in Frederiksted at the age of sixteen (16) as the valedictorian of my class—majoring in the commercial subjects of shorthand, typing, bookkeeping, business English, and business mathematics. This created perforce a period of joy—even euphoria at times—for my parents, my teachers, some of my close friends, and for me. But due to the stringency and anxieties of the times, we were soon to realize that the joy had to be taken in proper perspective—that we were experiencing times, which were marked by great disadvantages, albeit great opportunities for those who took a positive view of the situation and

Diploma from St. Patrick's Parochial School, June 25, 1933

accepted the times as challenges, barriers not to conquer but to be conquered.

The time was the peak of the Great Depression. Most people were out of work and wages were pitifully low, about twelve (12) cents an hour for unskilled people when you could get a job, which was rare. The bread lines of the National Recovery Administration (NRA) were long and depressing.

Housing conditions were deplorable by today's standards. They were a small throwaway from the slave standards, if at all. The buildings were inadequate in size, in the materials of which they were built, in architecture, and in convenience and economic layout. It seems that they were built not to accommodate and promote life but to make it difficult and miserable, to oppress and destroy it. Above all, the sanitation was horrible. The pit privy was preserved and revered as Lord and Supreme. It was conspicuous everywhere in more ways than to the eye.

At that point in time, graduating from the tenth grade was as far as you could go in Frederiksted. Indeed, even in Christiansted and Saint Thomas, the city fathers had just very reluctantly decided it was in the public interest to create a public high school. While the availability of secondary education is taken for granted today, in 1933, no one was sure that this would be a facility and opportunity available to all who qualified and were willing to take advantage of it. Certainly, it was still far away from Frederiksted, although it had barely made its advent in the capital city of Charlotte Amalie and Christiansted. Twelfth grade, or senior high school, graduation started in Saint Thomas only in 1931, with four graduates who included Enid Baa and Hugh Smith, who became two of Saint Thomas's great achievers. So in education, only junior high school education was available to the public in Frederiksted. That may be a good reason—how far we have come in educational opportunities available to the Virgin Islands public at public expense—why those of us who take maximum advantage of our secondary and college education available right here at home are wise indeed. It took long and hard work and lots of money to achieve these benefits for the public. To achieve it, most of the city fathers, who were at the time the landed gentry, had to be fought and overcome every inch of the way.

Health conditions were also quite bad. The infant mortality rate was about 50 percent. So a family with fifteen (15) children, like that of Peter and Wilhelmena Christian, was lucky if it saved eight, which it managed to do. The buildings used for hospitals and clinics were poorly designed, the special needs woefully inadequate, and the technical personnel just not provided. I remember walking in a line of about eighteen (18) youngsters to have my tonsils removed, then placed in a bed and fed okra fungi and fish the next day. The okra was added in liberal quantity to facilitate swallowing. I don't believe those practices would meet contemporary health standards.

As for the other public physical conditions, we have heretofore in this work related how undeveloped our road system was, the unlighted conditions of our streets, the absence of city public mains for salt or potable water, and the complete unavailability of public recreational facilities.

It is in this type of world I graduated from the tenth grade and began looking for work. But I had several things going for me, although I must confess I can see them better now, in retrospect, than I could in June 1933.

Indeed, the greatest thing I had going for me was the composite of the terrible conditions, which existed at the time but only, of course, if they were viewed as a challenge, a situation not to be conquered by but to conquer.

Then I had my own Roman Catholic religious faith, in a foolish and naive way perhaps, and the boundless hope based on that faith.

Another great asset I had going for me, as did millions of other people around the world, was the fact that Franklin Delano Roosevelt was just elected and inaugurated into office. True, the Depression had run its course, but separate and distinct from that fact was FDR, who inspired the mind and reanimated and refreshed the spirit of every man with his ringing declaration, "All we have to fear is fear itself." It was as if to sound the clarion call: Let's go to work with childlike faith and boundless hope!

Yes, the conditions prevailing in Saint Croix when I graduated did provide ample room for sober thought and opportunity for hard work, for struggle, to conquer, not only physical but also human and ideological obstacles. By making a reasoned comparison of the conditions, which prevailed in June 1933 with those same conditions as they exist today, the reader can draw his own conclusions of the progress made in these Islands of a national, territorial, insular, and personal dimension. As I look back, I feel personally proud and deeply gratified with the changes and improvements we have made under the Stars and Stripes. And I am not unmindful of the concomitant problems. But who can reasonably expect progress without paying some price?

CHAPTER VII

How I Came to Saint Thomas to Live

How I happened to leave Saint Croix at the age of seventeen (17) years and journey to Saint Thomas to work for the firm of A. H. Lockhart & Company Inc. (then headed by Mr. Herbert E. Lockhart Sr.) has always seemed a uniquely providential occurrence.

There were some very formidable personalities involved in this by contradistinction to myself. Mr. Lockhart was surely formidable enough in his very imposing and lofty personality, not to mention the fact that he seemed to be the beneficiary of the old English law concept of primogeniture. And while the vast patrimony of his recently deceased father, A. H. Lockhart—I did not go to him alone as the firstborn male child of the family—he looked and (I gathered at times) acted every bit the part of the sole recipient of that vast estate.

I am rather reliably told that when A. H. Lockhart died in 1931 in the heart of the Great Depression, he left an estate acquired by his labors—that is, no part of which was inherited—estimated conservatively at $4,000,000. Those who claimed he was the richest sole proprietor in the Territory at the time were probably right.

There was also my father, Peter Christian I, more commonly known as Boss Pete—a name he acquired from his many later-distinguished apprentices in carpentry, including Verne Plaskett, Cecil Williams, Harold Norman, and many others whose names I cannot remember. Some apprentices he had who did very poorly at his teaching of the trade were his own sons. I took one good look at the steep shape of a gable or hip galvanized roof topped by burning galvanized iron, sitting high up in the sky above two- and three-story buildings in the torrid sun, and instantly became petrified. I would work my pants off to make a living elsewhere.

Besides his vocation of carpentry, my father also had an avocation, farming hundreds of acres of land at Orange Grove and Anna's Rest Estates in Frederiksted. The biggest crop raised was sugarcane at a time when sugar was still king and the mainstay of the economy of the Islands. But we raised every imaginable type of tropical fruits, vegetables, and ground provisions. There was a plenitude of mangoes of every variety, eight or ten different species of bananas, carrots, radishes, beets, kohlrabies, pigeon peas, pumpkins, pineapples, yams, tannias, sweet potatoes, and so on. At times, we were short of money but never of native produce. There was always enough of that to spare, and unfortunately, much of it even lay around and spoiled.

The final character that had to do with my coming to Saint Thomas was the venerable Judge Denzil Noll. In those days, the Police Judge, which he was, could practice law when not in conflict with the performance of his judicial duties. In fact, this continued until seventeen (17) years later, when I was elevated to the same post of Judge of the Police Court, now the Territorial Court with vastly expanded jurisdiction. As judge and lawyer and white continental trained, Judge Noll's advice was just a euphemism for order.

A factor, which played a great role in the decision, was also the fact that I graduated at the top of my commercial class the year before, 1933—majoring in stenography, a not-too-widely-used business tool at the time. And Mr. Lockhart was so burdened with correspondence that he was rather receptive to seeing if someone, even though not so expert in the use of this tool, could lighten his burden and assuage his day.

Now Judge Noll happened to be the attorney of both A. H. Lockhart & Company and of my father. And one of his advices to both clients was to send me to Saint Thomas to serve as stenographer to Mr. Herbert, as we called him at the time. Don't ask me if I was consulted. It was 1934, not 1954 or 1974. As a young man of seventeen (17), still in my father's house, who had not even gone to a night dance as yet, I did as I was told. And as it turned out, I am happy that the filial relationship at the time produced that result.

My trip over on the *S S Catherine* did not serve to bolster my enthusiasm. As my first ocean voyage, perhaps aided by the deep uncertainty of how the new venture would turn out, it proved a cause of continuous illness from departure from Frederiksted Harbor to arrival at the West Indian Company Wharf. I need not describe the horrors of seasickness, but I had gone too far to turn back now. And besides, I was under orders from two very powerful men, my father and the old Lawyer and Judge.

CHAPTER VIII

My Three Years at the Firm of A. H. Lockhart & Co. Inc.

My joining the clerical, administrative, and executive staff at the firm of A. H. Lockhart & Co. Inc., was—at least in the beginning—a very traumatic experience. There were so many contrasts, or at least basic, sharp differences.

It was still the time before youth was lionized and enthroned or was almost automatically, if not supremely, accepted as definite entities, persons with rights. Instead, youths were still expected to be seen and not heard; to blindly obey, not to have any meaningful or respectable opinion on any subject; and to be content with being ignored. We have not yet arrived at a sensible middle ground between these two extremes. Surely, both sides could better mutually work together and achieve positive results at some point somewhere between these extremes.

I had just turned seventeen (17), while all my co-office workers ranged from thirty (30) to seventy (70).

These office holders came to work each day attired in a truly impeccable manner. They were dressed either in white drill or English linen with shirt, tie, and coat—indeed, sometimes with waistcoat too. Mr. Eduardo Moron (manager of Lockhart's prestigious department store, located in the center of the Main Street of the capital city of Charlotte Amalie) and Mr. Edward Faulkner (the stylishly mustachioed accountant at A. H. Lockhart & Co.'s lumberyard) added a special touch of class to this spiffy appearance by always appearing in spotless white shoes.

While this may not be as acute a factor today after the civil rights activism of the 1960s and the civil rights efforts of Dr. Martin Luther King Jr., President Kennedy, Robert Kennedy, President Johnson, et al., it was unusual to have a person of a complexion as dark as mine working in the front office as a stenographer. Indeed, it was revolutionary. One of your first qualifications for any job was not to be too dark, to be at least of a brown complexion. Qualify there first, then tell us what you can do. Even after I left the firm three years later, my color barred me from obtaining a job as a clerk or stenographer in any law office, private or governmental. Such was the mentality and negative mores of the times.

Another crass difference I had to encounter and adapt to besides age, dress, and color was with regard to names. As a stenographer, the problem of not seeming to have ever heard a long list of names thrown at me before was even greater than the ordinary, for it was not only a matter of hearing and understanding phonetically but spelling them correctly. And you know what misspelled word annoys anyone most of all. How dare you change my name? I had never heard of Lockhart, de Lugo, Christensen, Delinois, Paiewonsky, etc. Saint Croix names seemed completely absent from Saint Thomas residents. No Merwins, Flemings, Armstrongs, Williams, Christians, Plasketts, etc. I had to learn and adapt fast. Thank goodness, I survived.

The scope of business at Lockhart's during my three years was most interesting and invigorating, if only to contemplate. It was difficult to name a type of commerce in which this firm was not actively engaged. The general headquarters office where my boss, Mr. Herbert, worked oversaw dairy operations—including breeding, pasturing, and selling cattle and dairy products; real estate rentals with Charles Hay (manager) and William Lewis (chief building repairman); gas, oil, and other petroleum products of the West India Oil Co.; car sales, Packard (ask the man who owns one); the operation of a lumberyard offering all building materials with Kai Petersen, Mr. Lockhart's first son-in-law, as manager; dealing in alcoholic beverages of every description with a storeroom in the back of the office, (it was a delight to enter and savor the aroma of which smelled like the sweetest perfume); and steamship representation of the Bull Insular Line Inc., and the *SS Catherine* with fastidiously dressed Miguel Such as vice president. The firm of Lockhart was also agent for the manufacture and sale of every imaginable product and service in Europe and America. As the stenographer of A. H. Lockhart & Co. Inc., I can attest to the unbelievable range and number of the firms with which we corresponded.

And that brings me to two factors relative to my work that would be totally beyond the understanding of present-day workers. I was employed as a stenographer. As such, you would expect my work was to take dictation, transcribe, and perhaps file. This may have been the function for which only I was qualified, my specialty. But I was expected to do everything from selling gas at the pump on the sidewalk to finding the right type of liquor or cigarettes in the back store for an anxious customer in a hurry. And I was not only expected to do any and all manual work that I could manage but any and all office work that I knew, including assisting with the day-to-day bookkeeping. And I loved it. It gave me the opportunity for unlimited insight and growth in the world of commerce right from the heart of the most prestigious and perhaps richest firm in the United States Virgin Islands. Sure, the West Indian Company may have been more heavily capitalized, but Lockhart's was more diversified and was owned by a self-made native son and family. This was for me a deep sense of pride, inspiration, and motivation.

The other factor, though commonplace, that the present-day worker would not understand were the hours worked. We went to work at 7:30 a.m. and left when the boss elected to close the store, usually at 7:00 p.m. on ordinary days, but on tourist days and especially on Christmas Eve and Old Year's Night, at about midnight or later if the business kept coming. Hard? Perhaps. But it gave us the opportunity for a conditioning of body, mind, and spirit that could not be beaten or overcome by any ordinary adversity or adverse circumstances, which might confront us later in the endless and unforeseeable vicissitudes of this life.

I cannot stress too much the unlimited scope of the opportunity for growth, which my stint at the firm of Lockhart gave me. There were difficulties with adjusting to long hours; infinite variety of tasks to be performed; disparity of personalities to work with; rudeness and ribaldry of coworkers, which could not be avoided; etc. But in retrospect, generally, I gained immeasurably from this experience. And I certainly thank all who contributed to affording me this rich opportunity for growth and experience, even those who willfully created unnecessary crosses to be borne and overcome.

Later, when in 1951 I was confirmed as Judge of the now-Territorial, then-Police Court, Mr. Edgar Hall—my fatherly advisor and sage—put an unforgettable postscript on this whole experience. He said, "I regret only one thing today and that is that Mr. Herbert is not alive to see this."

CHAPTER IX

The End of My Work at Lockhart and the Experience I Had Immediately Thereafter

One may wonder how come I had such a rich learning experience at the Firm of A. H. Lockhart & Co. Inc., and yet decided to do all that was so painfully necessary to sever my connections on a permanent basis with so great and impressive an institution in the commercial and business community of Saint Thomas after only three years. Although at age twenty (20) I found this to be a rather difficult task to accomplish, I came to believe, despite the fact that I was gaining a considerable amount of knowledge at the firm, the conditions under which I worked, which I rightly or mistakenly deemed adverse were such as to plant and nurture in me over a sufficient period of time a strong determination not to stay permanently with the firm, albeit the most prestigious and affluent one in the Virgin Islands at the time, with the exception perhaps of the West Indian Co., Ltd., an offshoot of the East Asiatic Company.

I describe the greatness of the firm as lavishly as I do because it must be remembered that, although we are speaking of an era that was the early twilight of the Great Depression, this firm easily enjoyed a net worth of four to five million dollars, and it was all built by the business genius of one man, Alfred H. Lockhart I.

I do believe, also, that my leaving when I did—in spite of the strongest pressures and urgings exerted against it as we shall presently see—could have been greatly providential.

For the approximate period of three years that I clerked at the firm, I doubt I missed one day from work. And it must be borne in mind that these were not days when wages and hours were regulated by Government. You went to work when you were told by your employer to be there, usually between 7:00 and 7:30 a.m. and you left when the boss decided to call it a day. It was your duty to lock the main entrance door under the gaze of his penetrating eye.

But almost immediately as I delivered my notice of severance to Mr. Herbert, as we all called him, it became quite clear to me that I was in for a very difficult time. It appeared to me that while not so written explicitly anywhere I know of, it should have been understood by me that I did not decide that I would be employed by the firm (this had been done by others—Mr. Lockhart, my father, and Judge Denzil Noll, who was the attorney of both of these gentlemen). And therefore, I had no right to unilaterally decide to leave the firm. My attempt to do so seemed interpreted to be an act of unjustified temerity and impertinence and as such, had somehow to be nullified. In apparently thinking in this way and taking actions necessary to implement this thought, little weight appeared to be given to the fact of the constitutional right then already enshrined in the Organic Act of the Virgin Islands of 1936 that involuntary servitude shall not exist or be legal in the United States Virgin Islands. This was, of course, a very novel legal concept in the Territory. Theretofore, the practice was for a person to be employed by a firm at fourteen (14) or fifteen (15) and stay with the firm for life unless he was fired. But he had no right to leave on his own. In effect, he was an indentured servant.

While there was no violation of law committed by me by leaving the firm on my own initiative, this act clearly constituted a gross felonious assault on the revered employment practice of the day in that respect and something substantial had to be done to rectify the situation. It seems in retrospect that the course of conduct decided on to force me to undo the wrong I had committed was to approach it from the stark economic realities of the situation rather than from the legal stance, which was clearly not a viable one. After all, I had just come to Saint Thomas for the first time only three years before. I had no roots here. I was unpropertied, untitled, unknown, and had no family or other valuable educational, social, economic roots, or resources here. I had worked for $40 a month for the first year, $50 a month the second year, and $60 a month the third year, which was a very decent wage at that time in Saint Thomas but hardly enough to create any reasonable degree of economic security. So if the word were sent forth by a person as formidable and influential as Mr. Herbert up and down Main Street of the egregious infraction of the hiring-and-firing, age-old practice I had committed and that I should be taught a lesson for the good of myself and others similarly tempted. By no one employing me, I would be forced to return, beg pardon, and otherwise abide by the consequences. And the word did go forth accordingly.

And the word was faithfully heeded by all Main Street—all, that is, except one. Why there was this exception, I am not entirely certain. What I narrate here is based on hearsay, and while it sounds very plausible, I do not know it to be absolute fact.

I was told that as soon as the firm of A. H. Riise heard that I was being penalized in this way by the firm of Lockhart, they considered this the best justification to come to my rescue. They were responsible for giving me not one but two jobs. First, I was employed as stenographer and assistant bookkeeper, working under the immediate supervision of Ms. Ilma Crime and Mr. Louis Monsanto in the principal office of the firm of A. H. Riise.

My second job resulted from the fact that Ralph Paiewonsky (the darling son, the Little Flower of the firm, who was destined to be National Democratic Committee man and governor of the Virgin Islands for the second-longest term ever enjoyed in that prestigious job by any incumbent) was then in his freshman year as a member of the Municipal Council of Saint Thomas and Saint John. He was a very influential member of that August body, and they needed a stenographer. I was therefore employed to assist the then executive secretary of the body, Mr. Benito Smith, as stenographer to record verbatim the proceedings of the sessions of the local legislature and to assist with the stenographic and secretarial work in the office. Thus was brought to a close a tour of duty in the firm of A. H. Lockhart & Co., for which opportunity I will be eternally grateful for the training of the Roman Catholic Belgian nuns and Redemptorist fathers (mainly Father Edward Baumann, who gave me my early education; to my parents; and to Mr. Herbert Lockhart and his and my father's attorney, Judge Denzil Noll, who were truly among my most kind and valuable benefactors and teachers).

But I was also told why the firm of A. H. Riise would eagerly, openly, act in a manner clearly contrary to the wishes of the great firm of A. H. Lockhart and Company and the mores of the time.

A. H. Lockhart I was, without doubt, a business genius. From the modest winnings of a foreign lottery (I understand it was $10,000 first prize of the lottery of the Dominican Republic), he quickly rose to become clearly the wealthiest man in the Virgin Islands. As Providence would have it—money, property, worldly goods of every description—easily fell into his hands. Without a doubt, he had the Midas touch. But as he was getting on in his years, so the story goes, there were to him three valuable possessions he did not own and coveted. These are, as I am told an old local calypso ditty went, the Grand Hotel, the Apothecary's Hall, and John Brewer's Bay Estate. Alfred I was successful in acquiring the Grand Hotel, which is in the family's ownership to this day. But it was quite a different story when it came to acquiring the Apothecary's Hall, which at the time was owned by Isaac and Rebecca Paiewonsky. The considerable talent, indomitable will, and resilience of the Paiewonskies, especially that grand old lady Rebecca, were not to be overcome. Their genius, passion, and devotion to hard work constituted an impregnable obstacle to the realization of this goal by A. H. Lockhart I. This was the classic case of so good and so good, of stark power pitted against an immovable object. To this day, if the Paiewonskies do not own that property, it is only because they freely and voluntarily disposed of it.

To the keen observer, latent traces of the family feud and deep scars created by that confrontation persist socially, commercially, and even politically to this day. Yes, to this day, these families usually appear to stand at opposite ends of the political spectrum—or so it seems to this writer. I hope neither one will take offense to this observation, for I love them both and I could be wrong. But what is more important is the fact that both families are great pillars of the all-around strength and vitality of our Virgin Islands community, especially here in our beloved Saint Thomas.

I never learned what happened with respect to the ownership of John Brewers Bay Estate.

CHAPTER X

My Three Years after I Left the Firm of A. H. Lockhart & Co.: 1937 to 1940

Truly, 1937 to 1940 were years of groping—seeking to find my place by studying, holding many positions briefly, of political experimentation.

It is well to ask here: What happened to the two jobs you got from the Riise Firm? Well, they were very short-lived. This is because of a misplaced suspicion of then-Councilman Ralph M. Paiewonsky. In 1937, as stated earlier, he was a freshman councilman of the seven-member legislative council, which was the lawmaking body of the islands of Saint Thomas and Saint John, then constituting the political entity known and described as the Municipality of Saint Thomas and Saint John. He had been elected in what was the last election that was to be held of members to that council under the old voting system governed by income and property qualifications.

Why? Because on June 22, 1936, President Franklin D. Roosevelt signed into law the first Organic Act of the Virgin Islands, abolishing income and property qualifications as prerequisites for voting and giving to the masses, for the first time in our history, the right and power of the ballot. Henceforth, the only qualifications for the exercise of the right shall be citizenship in the United States, twenty-one (21) years of age, the ability to read and write English, and residence in the Islands for one year prior to the election. The political effect of this change was revolutionary. But it took some hard work to really make the change as far-reaching as it could be and became.

Some force had to come forward and point out to the nonvigilant and at times, somnolent masses the fact of the magnitude of the legal change made, its vast potentiality, and the need to take every advantage of it. Three men—and they were truly patriots, heroes of the masses, although we may not so recognize and honor them (Carlos Downing, Omar Brown, and Henry Richards) that is, a clerk of the police court and two small-time shopkeeper and not one of them hardly a freeholder or respected member of the landed class at the time—banded themselves together and founded the political party they called at the time the Progressive Guide of the Virgin Islands to attempt to organize, educate, and lead the newly enfranchised masses to take advantage of their new political power.

The new organization was being brought into being just at the time Hitler's and Mussolini's forces were being organized by them, and many avant-garde members of the opposition who could smell a rat at quite a distance derogated, defamed, and castigated the new group by likening it to recruits of Hitler's swastika and Mussolini's Blackshirts. They could see that the elitist control of the political life of the Islands held by them under the old system and presently in the hands of their Blue Party, or People's Party as they variously called themselves, was doomed to suffer a rather early demise.

They put up quite a fight. So dear and powerful and privileged a standing, held for so long, could not be relinquished without some struggle, albeit of easily predictable futility. So fight they did—in speeches, by slanders, gross calumnies, every trick in the book. But the one trick that would affect me was the mistaken rumor or silent campaign that every or nearly every young man who looked studious was one of those damn Guides. Apparently, someone had told Paiewonsky or he suspected that that fellow, Christian, was also a member of that notorious lot and since this was panic time, he must have swallowed it—hook, line, and sinker. But the truth was I did not even know of the passage of the 1936 Organic Act or of the organization or existence of the VI Progressive Guide.

But about six months after I got the two jobs, when I reported to work one morning at the office of A. H. Riise, I was told that because of retrenchments being made, they did not need my services anymore. Although this was late in 1937, when the recovery from the 1928–1932 Depression was well underway and I wondered and worried somewhat, I did not take it so hard. After all, I had my other job at the legislature and I was doing some private teaching of commercial subjects and some itinerant selling of wearing apparel, including shoes.

But within the hour—when I appeared at the office of the legislature and I got the heave-ho there, too—that was more than I could take without some real show of concern. The bad news there was given to me by the then executive secretary, Mr. Benito Smith. As I was walking out of the office, crestfallen, brokenhearted, he called me back and told me, "I cannot let you leave like this. I have to tell you it is Mr. Ralph. He thinks you are one of those Guide people who are against and working hard to replace the party now in power and you are a spy for their benefit."

Well, if you lose two jobs in one hour in a somewhat-bad economic time because you are suspected of belonging to an organization, the existence of which you even know nothing about, and you are only twenty (20) years of age, what is the most logical thing to do?

Checking out just who or what this VI Progressive Guide was, I came in contact with the militant firebrand Carlos Downing. After relating to him what happened to me, he could not be more pleased that they had brought him a new fired-up recruit. Downing said, "Come in with us, Alphonso. You are just the type of people we are looking for." Joining the Guide with some knowledge of office work and law resulted in a truly mutually beneficial partnership. I served as secretary, treasurer, vice president, president, and campaign manager and master of ceremonies in later political campaigns to the benefit of all its members, including Ralph Paiewonsky, as you shall see later.

While a member of the Guide between the years 1937–1940, I held positions in the police department and the public works department by the good graces of the late Adolph Gereau and Donald

S. Boreham. I also worked for the firm of the late Emile Berne in the shipping business. I served as a 1940 census enumerator for the Kronprindsens Quarter District and toward the end of 1940, served as a stenographer for the Arundel Company that built the Bourne Field fortifications during World War II.

By 1940 the efforts of the new political party, the Virgin Islands Progressive Guide, were so successful that from the three candidates that won election the first time they fielded a slate in 1938, they swept the entire slate of seven candidates into office by a landslide. The VI Progressive Guide had educated the newly enfranchised masses well on their newly won political power. The people had learned and appreciated their lesson well, and they had taken full advantage of the new power with which they had been vested very well.

And who is among the seven men swept into office on the ticket of the VI Progressive Guide in its landslide victory of 1940? He is one of the savviest politicians the entire Virgin Islands ever produced—no other than the Honorable Ralph M. Paiewonsky. But that is not all. His stature is such that politically, economically, and socially, he is so highly regarded by his legislative colleagues as to be invested as primus inter pares. He is made chairman of the new body upon its organization in January 1941.

By this time, old man Benito Smith is retired from age and because of politics, a change of party. And Chairman Paiewonsky is told by the other boys—his other six colleagues in the council—that

Alphonso A. Christian 1940

there has to be a rendezvous of fate and that their choice for the successor to Mr. Benito Smith as executive secretary is Alphonso A. Christian!

Did this meeting and reassociation create any difficulty? Absolutely not! It seemed to be made in heaven. Politics makes strange bedfellows. Mr. Paiewonsky and I got along handsomely. I found him to be a big man, not necessarily physically but in the ways where it counted—in spirit, in dealing with issues, in separating the things that really counted from those that didn't. Here is where I learned greatly from him. He was all for rewarding production wherever he found it.

When Ralph Paiewonsky retired from the Municipal Council of Saint Thomas and Saint John in 1946 and as a result thereof also from the Legislative Assembly of the Virgin Islands, which was the forerunner of our present unicameral legislature, I was truly sorry, for I knew we lost a great public servant. And the people no doubt generally agreed for he would come back, on appointment by President John F. Kennedy in 1961, to serve with rare distinction in the larger capacity as our governor fifteen (15) years later and to serve in that office longer than any other incumbent who preceded him there.

CHAPTER XI

My Entrance into Politics as a Member of the Progressive Guide and My Experience Therein, Especially with Several Members of the Legislature, Including a Majority and a Minority Bloc

Having been practically kicked into politics by that albeit-innocent suspicion of then-Councilman Ralph M. Paiewonsky—which was borne no doubt of his increasing sense of his own political insecurity and the obvious rapid eroding of his then-elitist, mainly Main Street constituency—I was in for some of the most telling experiences of my life.

I saw the nuts and bolts of how a political party has to be organized, administered, and kept alive; how to build an imposing and reliable political constituency; how to run a successful political campaign; what happens when you have defeated and routed all your outside political opposition; the constant, ruthless jockeying for name, position, and fame by the victors no matter how unpretentious their origins or because of that very fact; and the decline of the party as well as the fortunes of individual elected officials and the depths of despondency, melancholia, and utter diminishment of spirit, which became their sad and inevitable end.

Of course, the main beachhead of the Virgin Islands Progressive Guide, indeed its fountainhead, was the passage of the Organic Act of 1936 previously alluded to. But the crucial provision of that document that was more significant than all the other provisions put together—as far as the inspiration and motivation to create the new political party, which was to swiftly eclipse all its predecessors, was concerned—was that which gave the right and power of the ballot to the woefully deprived and destitute masses.

But the best law, the most potentially beneficial law, is only a dead letter unless it is detected, understood for exactly what it is and vigorously put into effect. And this is exactly the blueprint that Carlos Downing, Omar Brown, and Henry Richards quickly envisioned and set out to accomplish.

As long as the political windfall of the masses remained a dead letter, the existing powers went about their business and lived their lives in a business-as-usual manner. They could care less about the passage of the Act. But when they heard and really understood what the three theretofore unheard-of political nondescripts (veritable upstarts) intended to do with the Act, their blueprint for its maximum implementation and the far-reaching implications on the thus-far political birthright of the privileged seemed to have been hit with a surprise bolt of lightning. And political consternation—disarray and considerable disloyalty and in-house fighting and backstabbing—followed. They not only knew a rat when they saw it, but posthaste, they began to sniff at the sure prospect of their own demise—as a political tradition, era, and party.

But speaking hither and yon about the passage of the Act and what it meant with regard to the political power of the little man as he would be called from now on, no doubt to court his support and no less as a sort of euphemism, was only a crude beginning at best in bringing into fruition the successful creation of the new party. A constitution had to be drafted, studied, and passed. Who were eligible to become members, to remain members? How would the heretics and the infidels be expelled? What officers would the body have—their qualifications, powers, and terms of office? What committees would exist—their powers, officers, and terms of office? And finally, who would be eligible to run for legislative office to be the standard bearers of the party? For this was the jackpot—election as the legal representatives and the depository of the political power of the little man with authority to constitute and function as his lawmaking body.

Well, the constitution was drafted, studied, modified as thought necessary, and adopted.

The adoption of the constitution was quickly followed by every conceivable effort to build a strong, awesome, and enduring constituency. The somnolence of all segments of the little man heretofore in the entire history of the Virgin Islands—an established political fact since he never before enjoyed the right to exercise any political power—was ingrained and fossilized, not an easy fact of life to change. You don't change the history of centuries overnight. And remember, too, that these were poor people who needed the pittance they earned from their erstwhile, sometimes-present political bosses to keep body and soul together. So they must be very deft in exercising their newly endowed political power so as not to enrage the other side. Surely, they must be careful not to come out too quickly or openly or stridently in joining the new political menace, which has raised its ugly head like an ogre, a veritable menace, in our land. If they would be truly discreet, they would just register to vote and vote out the old guard—secretly and quietly on election day.

But the firebrands, although realizing the enormity and degree of risk of the task ahead, also were very confident that ultimately and in the not-too-distant future, victory was certain. And so they never feared or hesitated for a moment. In fact, they themselves did not have all that much to lose. Only Downing could lose his job as clerk of the police court, for Brown and Richards were independent, although small, shopkeepers. And it might backfire if the chief firebrand were fired because he was leading an all-consuming crusade to have the newly enfranchised underprivileged masses take advantage of their newly granted political rights.

Would such a spiteful, malicious, and retaliatory act not elevate Downing to a state of political martyrdom, make a popular hero of him, and now really make certain the rapid demise of the Blue Party? While such an act may well have been given considerable thought by the men in deep and solemn council, to their everlasting credit, there were wiser heads among them who no doubt vetoed the idea. For Carlos Downing served until he decided to quit his post and turn it over to his protégé, Alwyn Lad Richards.

The Progressive Guide decided to aggressively build and consolidate its constituency by appealing wherever men were, even to their inborn prejudices, to get votes. Appeals were made from every soapbox, restaurant, in every church where they would be allowed, not to mention in the residences of all who would admit them—to educate, woo, enlist. All races and classes were appealed to—Blacks, Whites, Mixed, Frenchies, Puerto Ricans. All the crass and not-so-crass abuses of the ever-so-long, brutal, ugly past were unearthed and brought into focus for all to remember, to contemplate, to decry, and to vow to bring to a screeching halt.

Meetings at headquarters were held two and three times a week to rally and reassure the faithful and to swear in wave after wave of new recruits. Speech after speech was made by the leaders and down the line to reassure all that we were on the right path. And when reassurance was thought necessary from the outside, formidable personalities—such as the late Judge William H. Hastie, the late Judge Herman E. Moore, and the late Attorney James A. Bough—were brought in to address, inspire, and motivate the membership. It was not unusual for these meetings to last into the wee hours of the morning. This was indeed a veritable crusade!

And if any traitors were found or suspected (and aren't there always some of these?), steps were taken to try to expel them. In fact, before one became a member, he had to be investigated, found to be in tune with the new political philosophy found in the Constitution, and had to be formally initiated and pay a fee into the new party. Unlike the present practice begun by statutory enactment in 1963, one could not become a member of the Virgin Islands Progressive Guide by just stating he wished to and sign a simple application to that effect. Initiation, becoming a Guide involved a rather thorough process, ensuring above all that you understood and subscribed to the new political philosophy and could be truly relied upon and trusted to support and nurture and promote it. And once in, if you wished to stay in, you had to conduct yourself above reasonable suspicion—not just avoiding scrupulously all evil but also, as Caesar's wife, the reasonable appearances thereof. However, you could not be expelled because of mere baseless suspicion, or arbitrarily, but only by the observance of a duly adopted legal process that was evenhandedly applied to all members.

Indeed, as a result of the 1936 Organic Act, the dream, the political organization, and the aforesaid administration—when the Party, after only a short year in existence, ran its first slate of seven men in 1938—it elected three to the seven-member legislative council. Only encouragement could flow from such a remarkable result. And by 1940, when the Party ran its second slate, its efforts paid off beyond all reasonable expectations, for it elected all the seven members of the local legislature by a landslide.

Now that every foe was vanquished, we would fight among ourselves for the spoils of victory. Who would chair the body, the committees, be sent on trips to Washington and elsewhere? Fights over these and other matters could be very bitter, selfish, greedy, and divisive. And one of the worst results was the division of the seven-member council into a four-member majority bloc and a three-member minority bloc, and these blocs divided even the small-by-today's-standards office staff along the same lines.

As to the fate of the party, it seems when you are on top, you can go only in one direction and that is down. So it may well be that the infighting was inevitable. And it surely was politically fratricidal, first to individual members—Hill, Harris, Gordon (Ralph Paiewonsky declined to run in 1946), and finally, Omar Brown in 1952. Indeed, when their political star had run its course, many of them spoke as if they rued the day they decided to become politicians. Many times when they walked on Main Street, former political enthusiastic supporters would look the other way or turn their backs or even quickly change sidewalks. One politician who experienced this kind of treatment told me it made him feel as if his soul had suddenly left him. But all politicians—except those who have the sense and the courage to know, when to say stop, and to wisely heed that advice—pass this same way and suffer this same rather very sad fate.

Thus, in 1952, the fourteen (14)-year era of a great work, a great party, and the service of great servants of the people came to an end. We had established for the foreseeable future a new political life for the Islands, controlled the local legislature for seven consecutive terms or a fourteen (14)-year period, and in the process, had made a giant change in the political, educational, economic, and social life of all the people of the Virgin Islands. Thus was the life and era of the Virgin Islands Progressive Guide, founded by Carlos A. Downning, Omar Brown, and Henry V. Richards. These three men contributed greatly to the well-being and uplift of their contemporaries as well as posterity. We as Virgin Islanders will forever be in their debt. May God bless them!

CHAPTER XII

My Study of Law and My Admission to the Bar after Two Tries: One Unofficial and One Official

As a stenographer writing the Gregg system of shorthand, I subscribed to *The Gregg Reporter*. This was a periodical written in Gregg shorthand and longhand designed to upgrade the skill of the Gregg writer as a stenographer and enhance his knowledge of commercial and office work in general. In one of these periodicals, I came upon the inspirational statement that shorthand is a powerful means of opening the door to unlimited knowledge, for the stenographer has the unique privilege of writing down verbatim and understanding and transcribing in good, intelligible, readable form the thoughts and concepts of the best minds in the country, indeed of the world. And I was at the time recording and transcribing the thoughts of one of the richest and most influential men in the Virgin Islands, Herbert E. Lockhart. (Pardon me, I never found out what the E stood for). Soon, too, Mr. Herbert would have me record the thoughts, both lay and legal, of his attorney, Judge Denzil Noll.

Hearing the terminology, the nomenclature of the law, for the first time under circumstances—which made it imperative that I listen closely, understand, and record what I heard accurately—planted in me what was to become an unquenchable love for the law and its whole language and convinced me of the probability of the truth of that statement in *The Gregg Reporter*. I became determined to at least make a serious attempt to engage in the study of the law. It was to be a long and arduous yet very rewarding endeavor.

It was the year 1934, early in a decade, which was to be great in its ambitious—sometimes Byzantine—undertakings to recover from the Great Depression of 1928–1932 to achieve, amass, and hold on to political power. And the great world figures of the thirties may never have been equaled in any succeeding decade to date—Franklin D. Roosevelt, Winston Churchill, Adolf Hitler, Joseph Stalin, Chiang Kai-shek, Charles deGaulle, and Joe Louis to name a few. Those were the early days of radio (television had not yet come on the world scene), and when any of those men were involved in a broadcast, it was always a very special event to be looked forward to and definitely not to be missed—if not worldwide, certainly not in their particular country.

I was also motivated by a third factor, which I referred to earlier. My father—speaking and acting as if the big Depression would last forever when he was asked to send me to college after I graduated as the valedictorian of my class in 1933—refused, stating that there were lawyers and doctors walking the streets of New York hungry. Why should he waste money to add another one to that hapless lot? If I could—by dint of hard work and employing that greatest of the virtues of success and perseverance—pull it off, become an attorney, and succeed at it, I would really prove to him just how wrong (and maybe selfish) he was.

So with all three motivations as a catalyst and my launching pad, I enrolled in correspondence course number one for the study of law in 1936 at the American School of Law to better understand what they described as The American Technical Society. It was a three-year course, which I completed on schedule. Even without being prepared according to the then-prevailing rules to be admitted to sit the bar exam, I was handsomely rewarded. My vocabulary, both lay and legal, swelled considerably, helping me to more readily understand and accurately take dictation related to commerce and the law. I was better prepared to participate in the burgeoning activities of the new and fast-growing political party of the late thirties, the VI Progressive Guide. And when I was employed part time as stenographer to record ad verbum the proceedings of the local legislature, I could understand with considerably more ease the terminology so common to that body and their official environment. And my greater usefulness in these areas made me more acceptable and appealing to the powers of that day in the legislature, the political party, even in the many and varied business offices of the day where I worked.

But the culmination of that first course of study of the law involved the actions of two very influential men. So impressed with my efforts in that respect was Mr. Conrad Corneiro (then the honorable chairman of the Municipal Council of Saint Thomas and Saint John, which was the local legislature, the lawmaking body, of the Municipality of Saint Thomas and Saint John as distinguished from the Municipality of Saint Croix, according to the Organic Act of June 22, 1936), who was willing to introduce and attempt to have enacted by that body what we would quickly recognize today as a private special act—to have me admitted to the local bar. Obviously, this being special legislation, it was illegal. But all the way back then, our legal thinking was not as sophisticated as it is today, and therefore, his mention of the idea was not regarded as being so startling, repulsive, inconceivable, indeed unacceptable as it would be today. What counts really is the bottom line that the special bill was never introduced, let alone passed.

The other big official who became involved was our then-sitting federal district court judge, the Honorable Herman E. Moore. While Chairman Corneiro did not proceed to try to help me in his legislative branch of the government, he advised me to put the matter before Judge Moore in the judicial branch. I was only twenty-three (23) years of age at the time with relatively scant either formal training or experience. The good judge was kind to me. He reviewed the case and told me how favorably impressed he was with my ambitions and efforts to date but added that frankly, I was not ready. But he advised me, in fact urged me, to press on. And how right he was! What good advice he gave me! I decided I would do my best to heed his words of wisdom, not knowing that ten years later, almost to the day, he would be the very official to say well done, etc.

I did not have all the time in the world to follow Judge Moore's advice to press on in the study of the law. I found myself loaded with burdens: I became executive secretary of the legislature; got married and began fathering, raising, and educating my children; represented a firm named Haas Brothers in California that sold foodstuff wholesale; was court reporter for the Army courts-martial at Camp Harwood located at the West Indian Company during World War II and for visiting congressional committees; engaged in the building of my first house at No. 1 Nye Gade; and also ran a private school, teaching shorthand, typing, business English, business math, and stenotypy. I also held one high office or another in the Progressive Guide and when the political opposition became a real threat, acted as master of ceremonies at all political rallies in all political campaigns in which the VI Progressive Guide was involved from 1944 through 1950.

So because of competition for my time, the study of law was, as it were, squeezed onto the back burner. But the political campaign of 1948 would change all that. When the late great William H. Hastie first came to the Islands, he was sent here as federal district judge, the first Black to hold that position in the United States or its territories. This was in 1937, the year the VI Progressive Guide was born. Judge Hastie was fascinated and most enthused with what the Guide was trying to accomplish to give full effect to the provisions of the newly enacted Organic Act of 1936, especially those provisions enfranchising for the first time in history the large underclass or masses of the Islands and generally to breathe life into the new Act, which by coincidence, he was instrumental in drafting. He therefore did everything he could, consistent with the requirements and constraints of his high office, to counsel and pilot the Guide to success in its ambitious, humanitarian, and historic undertaking. And the Guide succeeded handsomely as we reported earlier in these memoirs.

But Judge Hastie left this post and the Virgin Islands after only two years to become special assistant to the Secretary of War during World War II.

Alphonso A. Christian I, (center) as stenographer to record ad verbum the proceedings of the local Legislature in 1945

When Judge Hastie returned in 1946, he was now the Governor of the Virgin Islands; he had a new wife, Beryl (Lockhart) Hastie; and he was to espouse a more conservative political philosophy. It seemed that he believed he had helped to create, father, and make powerful—indeed too powerful—a Frankenstein monster. And regrettably, he would now be forced in the public interest to do all he could to bring about its demise. He first worked with the rebellious fringe within the Guide itself—then presumably headed by Earle B. Ottley (who, at the time, was a young, vigorous, bright newspaper publisher) and Valdemar Hill (former member of the legislative council)—to form a new party to fight and if possible, destroy the VI Progressive Guide. The new rival party ran its first full slate of candidates in the 1946 campaign. All its candidates, except its leader, Mr. Ottley, went down to an ignominious defeat.

This may have stunned them, but it did not stop them. They reorganized, regrouped, and began almost immediately, planning to recharge for a knockout blow in the 1948 campaign. But there were some preliminary softening-up steps to take. Along the way, a scandal suit was instituted against the biggest vote getter of all Guide legislators—the Honorable Omar Brown, the first elected member at large—charging him with stealing gasoline. The other member at large—the Honorable Ralph Paiewonsky, who did not stand for office at the end of this 1944–1946 term—was replaced by the Honorable Carlos A. Downing. All the forces of the executive branch and a hostile, if not jealous, press were thrown into the fray against Brown and the Party. But when the jury verdict was in, he was unanimously acquitted. Omar was ably represented by one of the ablest defense counsel around at the time, Attorney David Maas.

Next, a quo warrant to suit was instituted by the Governor himself with the aid of his protégé, then the United States Attorney Francisco Corneiro, and prosecuted by the Governor himself as a lawyer in court to have decided the issue. "By what right do members of the legislature sit and function as members of executive or administrative boards and commissions in the light of the American doctrine of the separation of powers now ingrained in the newly enacted 1936 Organic Act made applicable to the Islands on June 22, 1936?"

The Governor won that round.

Thirdly, Hastie had served as governor of the Virgin Islands for nearly three years by election eve 1948 and was looked up to as a great governor and an idol among his Black folk, the major political voting constituency in the Islands. So on this election eve, the Governor has just flown back from campaigning on the Mainland for the election of President Harry S. Truman to give what was certain to be a knockout speech against this brainchild that had become too big for its breeches, too naughty, and most intractable. Just a good spanking would not do. Total eradication, elimination, was absolutely necessary. President Truman had visited the Islands in 1946, was well-loved here, and was then seeking a full term to the presidency in his own right. It will be remembered that Truman was FDR's vice president in the latter's fourth term; succeeded FDR when the president died in office in April 1945; and promptly appointed Hastie governor of the Islands to succeed Charles Harwood, who heard the bad tidings while on one of his frequent airplane trips back to the Mainland. All these factors were bound to give added weight and thrust to Hastie's urgent call for the eradication and demise of this spoiled child, the Virgin Islands Progressive Guide.

It was in this highly charged and built-up background and context that all the candidates of the VI Progressive Guide for reelection to the legislature learn on the morning of that fateful 1948 election eve that the great Governor William H. Hastie would be the keynote speaker for the opposing party (called the Liberal Party) at Roosevelt Park to unseat all the rascals, for which most important undertaking he flew back especially to the Islands on the precise appointed day. The catchphrase, or slogan, of the Governor's speech before a record ten thousand (10,000) or so listeners, which started at 8:00 p.m. was "Let's throw the rascals out!" The program was enthusiastically received, especially by those who, during the past ten years and five political campaigns, had been beaten by "the rascals." Now, finally, their day of revenge had come. But did it really?

All the candidates and workers, including this writer, as campaign manager, listened to the whole big show at Roosevelt Park. As soon as they bade the huge crowd "Good night. See you at the polls tomorrow," we ascended the platform from which our friends had departed posthaste and we invited all the listeners to come down to the Emancipation Garden to hear our side *and be emancipated from the big conspiracy.* It was about 11:00 p.m., but they came by the thousands and they listened and cheered from 11:00 p.m. to 4:00 a.m. election day. And when the votes were cast and counted, the VI Progressive Guide had won a resounding victory. The only member of the opposition who survived a crushing defeat was, again, Earle B. Ottley. Ralph Paiewonsky observed his paper saved him, implying by the skin of his teeth.

But the most painful part for the beloved Governor Hastie was he was standing before this writer, who was the caller of the votes, in the police courthouse in Fort Christian and he must have been sickened by the resounding, unending cacophony of the call of the names of the Guide candidates for reelection. The widely held and accepted rationale for his defeat was that the electorate resented

58

an appointed (not elected) governor attempting to dictate to them whom they should elect to their legislature. It was the only branch in the formation of which they had a voice, especially when he had just preached to them by taking their elected legislators to court—how sacred the separate functioning of those branches was in our democratic form of government—by virtue of the long-respected and honored doctrine of the separation of powers. The voters were wise and discerning enough not to accept this duplicity, even from their idol.

But what does all this have to do with my study of the law? It all threw a terrible scare in me. Suppose the opposition had succeeded? I returned to the second course of law I was then studying, now with LaSalle Extension University, with passionate vigor and dedication. When I completed the course in November of 1949 and received my diploma, I again applied to Judge Moore for admission to the Bar. This time, he adopted a motion, permitting me to sit the exam. And there was no happier man than the judge, except me perhaps, when I was victorious. Other jubilant and proud and grateful people were my father, my old boss (Mr. Herbert), Ralph Paiewonsky (who I believe played no small part in my good fortune), and of course, my wife, Ruth (who many, many times felt and fretted aloud that the books were winning the competition with her for my time and attention).

CHAPTER XIII

My Family Life

I came from a very large Catholic family. My mother told me at age nineteen (19), she was courted and taken out of the home of her parents (Alexander and Theresa Benjamin) in marriage to my father (Peter Christian I) at age twenty-five (25) in the Roman Catholic Parish Church of Saint Patrick in Frederiksted. She also told me that they begot fifteen (15) children, only eight of whom survived infanthood due to the extremely high rate of infant mortality of her day. My parents lived together for fifty-four (54) years, my father passing in 1957 at age seventy-nine (79) and my mother at age eighty-seven (87) in 1970, both in their home Island of Saint Croix.

By the time I was sent to Saint Thomas in 1934 to work as stenographer to Mr. Herbert E. Lockhart, I had been the beneficiary of the maturing, refining development that was the blessed legacy of any children who grow up in a closely knit, large family, which was Christian centered, prayed together, and worked together under the love and disciplining of stern parents—in our case, especially my father. I had learned the value of give and take in life; of suffering patiently, even stoically, without undue whining and complaining; to live and let live; and to sift the important from the trivial. In a word, that innate ability, training, and hard work were not enough for success but having and always displaying the right character and attitude was also an indispensable ingredient of any man who really intends to make it in life. In more sophisticated and erudite circles, in sociological language, the coming together and practical interaction of all these four qualities is usually referred to as effective social adjustment.

It seems that my large Catholic family in Saint Croix was just the perfect background and foundation for the family life I would be heir to in Saint Thomas. Here, I was originally placed with the Hughes sisters to board. These were two lovely spinsters who lived near Saints Peter and Paul Cathedral. These ladies (God bless them) were very kind to me, even to take me into their fine home and in assisting me to make the great family and social adjustments, which the change from living in Frederiksted (a small, agricultural, isolated community) to Saint Thomas (a comparatively sophisticated, commercial community) entailed. These changes included not only social but also educational, racial, cultural, and financial ones.

I have often been persuaded that unless Father Edward Baumann, the Superior at Saints Peter and Paul at the time (1933–1939), had interceded on my behalf, these ladies would never have opened their beautiful home and extended their kindnesses and hospitality to me. Now, I would need all the strength of all the positive attributes I gleaned from my family life in Saint Croix, especially that of always displaying the right character and attitude, to make this relationship work. They had done their part. It was now up to me to do mine. I will always be grateful to my parents, grandparents, the Redemptorist Fathers, and the Belgian Sisters for the preparation they gave me, which played so great a role in preventing my first experience of life in Saint Thomas with the Hughes sisters in 1934 from being a complete disaster.

By 1941—when I married Ruth and Reubina and Alicia, her two daughters of eleven (11) and six years of age, respectively—I was twenty-five (25) years of age and must have lived in ten places, some as a boarder in the homes of others and some as a bachelor in my own home.

But you ask, "What do you mean when you say you married Ruth and her two daughters?" Well, it is my view that when one marries anyone, he also marries their immediate family, especially the

61

children of their body. If you doubt it, try dealing with a mother of
stepchildren without taking
their every position into account.
Or conversely, try dealing with
the stepchildren without the
fullest accountability to their
mother.

Indeed, the mother of stepchildren is even more sensitive
about everything her husband
does relating to those children
than about his actions touch-
ing the children both of them
beget. She is wont to take a most
impossible position. If the step-
father is strict with the stepchildren, it is because they are not
the issue of his body. If he is
indifferent or even lenient with
them, well, he just does not care

Newlyweds – Alphonso
& Ruth—1941

what happens to them because they are not his children. It is a most
difficult, indeed a no-win, situation. So if you are facing the possibil-
ity of marrying someone with children, who are still minors, think
very carefully if you are prepared to deal with what usually is a most
trying, if not untenable, situation.

By the grace of God, Reubina survived to be a very fine, well-ad-
justed person who loves me more today—I am sure of it—than she
did while growing up under my roof. And Alicia (my second stepchild) has been blessed with a fine education, an outstanding husband (who practiced law in his native Philadelphia), and three lovely,
well-educated children. So all of us did overcome, somehow, the
inevitable ambivalence and intrinsic difficulties of step parenthood
notwithstanding.

I should say a word of my housing situation and experience
when I got married and how that situation changed in time. At marriage, Ruth having two daughters aged eleven (11) and six years living

with her, we had an immediate need for housing for a family of four. I was living at the time in a small second-story building belonging to Jens Tangaard (optician, jeweler, and real estate investor), which was located above a gas station facility at the eastern end of Main Street. It consisted of one bedroom, a parlor, a drop shed used for entrance and dining, a kitchen, a small bath, and a tiny porch. Quite adequate for a bachelor but obviously not so adequate for four persons.

I reasoned that instead of moving to expensive, more adequate accommodations, I should stay put for a while, attempt to save a little money, then spend my money to own rather than to rent a good, comfortable home.

But Ruth saw it differently. She married to improve her lot in life and she wanted that improvement now, not possibly later. So we had our first marriage crisis within months of the wedding. And had it not been for another serious social obstacle, I would have given in to Ruth. This obstacle, in time, would prove to be a blessing in disguise.

In the early 1940s, a classless, relatively unknown, poor Black person was plain naive to think he could rent a decent house for the use of his family—no matter what he could afford to pay. This was anathema to the landed gentry and land barons of that not-so-ancient era. So no matter how I tried (and I tried hard) to get a nice house to rent with say two or three bedrooms, it was impossible. That was the bad side of the matter. The good side of it was the opportunity it forced upon me to have some extra money, to really save some money—especially since both Ruth and I were working, I at three or four jobs.

But several new developments made it mandatory for me to move. The manager of the gas station needed our quarters for his own personal use and began what appeared to be a planned campaign of harassment to make us move. So effective was his sinister, ruthless plan and overt behavior that Ruth became ill as a direct result of it. Whether her illness was due to her undue sensitivity or to the intensity of the irritation or both, I cannot tell, but the fact of her illness was something to which I had to give my very immediate attention. Then secondly, our first child, Barbara Theresa, was born around this time—with its obvious effects on Ruth's health, the need for more space, and the effect of the entire situation on the postpartum well-being of the child. And how anxiously we had looked forward to having our first child! And how lovely she was! I remember her first cousin—the late Alma Heath of blessed memory, twin sister of Dr. Alfred O. Heath—remarking on first seeing Barbara only weeks after her birth, "She is so beautiful!" Surely, I could not risk exposing the health of Ruth and Barbara to the adverse factors we were suffering from living in this house.

But we still could not get a suitable house to rent. Conditions had not changed much in two years. So in desperation, we moved to another house (a two-room house) for some respite from the harassment, albeit the space accommodations were as bad or worse. We would stay here only until we could find better, even if not adequate, quarters.

While here, we were told that one Emile Hodge had just built a modern, cottage-type house on Nye Gade. We eagerly and promptly went to see it and found that luckily, while it was not ideal, at least it was new, modern, clean, and had two bedrooms. And most importantly, we can have it. It was while I was in this house that I saw and obtained the opportunity of building my first home (Number One Nye Gade), which was, at the time, the old ruin of a family great house of a former era. This ruin was located just below my present rented residence and had been placed by its owner (Ariel Melchoir Sr., at the time editor and publisher of the *Virgin Islands Daily News*) in the hands of his lawyer at the time (the late Attorney George H. T. Dudley) for sale. The savings—which the rental policies of the land barons of the day forced upon me motivated me to make—now came in very handy. I was able to pay $1,500 cash for the property. And I wasted no time planning and commencing the reconstruction and renovation of the property to provide a home for my family and two more apartments, which I rented to persons similarly situated. The venture turned out to be a true winner—a three-residence rather comfortable and commodious apartment house solidly built so that, with reasonable care, it should last for many generations to come.

#1 NYE
GADE

First home and location where Barbara, Alphonso II, and Cora were
delivered by Nennie Eugenie Forde, our midwife, and neighbor

In my next chapter, I shall give an account of how the bitterness
generated in me by the prejudice, which prevailed in renting premises at the time—at the time of my marriage—motivated and created in me a burning passion to build a really beautiful home for
my family, as contradistinguished from an apartment house, and to
become a respectable freeholder in my own right. Thank God indeed
for blessings in disguise! If one bears his crosses with a positive attitude, with a determination to overcome them rather than allowing
them to overcome him, one never knows into what blessings he will
not convert them.

CHAPTER XIV

The Housing Situation in the Islands and How It Forced Me to Struggle to Own My Own Home

Contemporary society complains about the inadequacy of the housing conditions in the Virgin Islands today (during the nineties), both as to quality and quantity, and they have ample justification for their complaints. But if they really knew what the housing conditions were up to the 1950s, they would get a true perspective of how very, very far we have progressed in this respect in the past three or four decades.

The housing conditions were extremely bad in that there were just not sufficient habitable units for the population of the forties, although small when compared to the population of today. Since the forties, the population has more than tripled, from a mere thirty thousand (30,000) or so to approximately one hundred thousand (100,000) in the nineties.

The situation was even worse when we see what, in fact, was considered and accepted as a habitable unit. For the vast majority of the people, which ran anywhere near 90 percent, that meant an old, almost completely superannuated frame one- or two-room building in cramped quarters with old galvanized or felt roof—often porous, both on the top as well as on the sides—so you could both feel and see from the inside when it was raining. There was little privacy from the inquisitive eyes of nonoccupants of your dwelling or protection from the constant invasion of rodents, roaches, termites, ants, mosquitoes, centipedes, bugs, the relentless heat of the tropics, and other pests—a veritable torture chamber.

As a result of the crowded conditions, many children lived and slept packed like sardines in one room. They slept on what was called lodgin', which was old clothes and other worn-out clothes spread on the floor, sometimes when they were lucky, on pieces of board laid out on boxes. Sometimes to give the usually unpainted, dark, dank room a new, more cheerful look of sorts, at Christmas, Easter, and Pentecost time, they would paper the walls with the pages of Walter Field, Montgomery Ward, and other mail order house catalogs using white flour paste mixed with an extract from the locally called simtiwiby (correct spelling semperviva) plant for glue.

There was not, in most cases, even a decent pit privy or outhouse if indeed there could be such a thing by modern American sanitary standards. Thus, for most dwellings, especially those used by tenants, there was the infamous night soil removal service whereby the government periodically sent trucks with crews from neighborhood to neighborhood at night to remove the accumulated human waste gathered in cans placed in the various properties or in pits for that purpose.

Where pits existed for the accumulation of the stuff, no cans were usually necessary or used. In my father's property, Number Forty Prince Street in Frederiksted, I remember well the trips of the pit cleaners hired by him to clean the toilet. You could always hear them as they did their sordid but most essential task, moving back and forth the length of the property from the street to the utmost rear, about one hundred (100) feet distance, where the pit was located. And even if you did not hear them, you had to smell them at work. But in any event, there was no escaping clear and conclusive proof of their presence the day after. There were unmistakable vestiges of their labor all over the property. Thank God, after a long and determined battle waged by the Virgin Islands Progressive Guide and many American executive administrations, this most unpleasant, obnoxious, repulsive phase in our history is behind us.

Of perhaps a less repugnant, although also quite worrisome nature, was the water supply. It all came from rooftops, wells, springs, or guts in the Danish times. Later, the American executive administrations added water catchments on the sides of hills with cisterns or reservoirs below and standpipes by and from the reservoirs to serve the water needs of the neighborhood residents. This marked the beginning of availability of running water for the masses. The water, when available, was not piped into homes but to street corners when the neighborhood residents queued up to collect their share.

The neighborhood well was the forerunner of the neighborhood standpipe and tap. Large numbers of residents, especially in the town areas where access to live springs and guts did not exist as in the rural areas, had the water from their well supplemented by collection in drums and barrels from rainfall, especially where there was no cistern in the yard of the property in which they lived. Many folks say that in those days of relatively primitive means of meeting the water needs of the people, there was less scarcity of water than today when we boast many of the advancements of modern life. But were the people as educated to the need to use as much water for their health and well-being? Did they not have to carry every drop they used rather than have it powered to them by electricity or gravity? Were our forebearers as educated as we are today as to the acceptable quality of water to use, especially for drinking and bathing, to maintain good health? Aren't there three to four times the population to be provided with a much greater amount of water of better quality for each resident on a permanent basis? My humble opinion is that these people may be comparing apples with oranges.

This review of the housing condition would be woefully incomplete in these days of the malaise of the Water and Power Administration (WAPA) if I did not say a word about electric power as it affected the housing condition of the thirties and forties. In a word, there was, for all practical purposes, no electric power to speak about. First, we had direct current (DC), also dubbed Danish Current, to distinguish it from AC—alternating current, also dubbed American Current. DC quickly came to be regarded as one of the curses of the local scene to be gotten rid of as soon as possible. Indeed, one of the first objectives tackled by the VI Progressive Guide—which was the first political party to take advantage and enjoy the benefits of election to power by the masses as they became enfranchised for the first time in our history by the passage of the 1936 Organic Act—was the elimination of DC current. This issue had the dubious distinction of being one of the principal planks of their platform.

To illustrate how few people enjoyed electric power and the quality or lack thereof in the 1930s and 1940s, I will relate an incident I will never forget that happened in this connection in my father's house in 1932. That was the acquisition by my folks for the first time of electric power in the house. That acquisition was marked by the proud and special completion of the installation of a single bulb light in the center of our little sitting room, hanging on a fly-ridden electric cord. My mother, all the children, and some of the tenants were invited to witness the great event. Naturally, the only person who was allowed to use it was the old man, not even my mother, let alone the rest of us.

But it was not only the overall lack of sufficient, habitable housing with adequate sanitary facilities, water, and power that plagued the population as late as the thirties and forties. More repulsive was the social attitude.

Even if you were lucky enough to earn enough to afford to buy or rent a decent home, if you did not belong to a traditionally acceptable class, you could forget it. You were forced to live on such a substandard level, not as your means made necessary or inevitable but according to the mold in which the landed gentry, the land barons, placed you. This mold was affected by the family you came from, your education, your race, your color, and of course, your economic level. Qualify in all these and other respects and you are in. Fail to qualify in any one of these many respects, most of which were and inherently are not of your making and beyond your control, and you are just a social pariah, an outcast, at least as far as being able to obtain a decent house in which to live and raise your family is concerned. Did it matter if you could afford and would pay the rent or price? No. Or that you would take good care of the premises? No. Or that you would be an otherwise good tenant or neighbor, easy to get along with? Absolutely not.

When I got married in 1941 and was confronted with this social condition, I fell into a state of melancholia and remained there for days, weeks. Then I gradually came to the realization that perhaps this was just the kick in the pants that I needed to jolt me into putting forth the effort, Herculean though it might be, to become independent of these people, to defy and rise above this odious tradition. And I then and there resolved that no matter how long it took me, or how much effort and sacrifice it took, I would one day build, own, and live in a house, which was better than many of the houses I was prevented from even renting. And in 1946, five years after my resolution, I succeeded in moving into such a house, my first home, at No. 1 Nye Gade.

Alphonso II and Cora on porch of #1 Nye Gade

And even then, one of these land barons, a councilman with whom I was working in the Municipal Council, had the temerity to admonish me that I should not move into the newly finished top floor of my own house but I should rent it to one who fitted the mold of the old days. This suitable man was making much less income than Ruth and I were, but no matter. Based on the standards and traditions of the past and of this councilman, it would be a major heresy for me and my family of four to move into this new creation. Since I was working with and to some extent, under him, I only said I would think about it and proceeded to ignore him and to live according to my resolution.

After Nye Gade, we proceeded to build my present dwelling house at No. 16 Solberg, which more than fulfilled my resolution of 1941, although it cost me my first incumbency as a judge—my judgeship of the Police Court. Other reasons were given, but when I reviewed the history that began in 1952 and culminated in 1954 with my removal, I reached the inescapable conclusion that had I not attempted to rise above my socially imposed britches and built the mansion on the hill (the Baronial Hall as one of my friends dubbed it), I would not have been removed from that position at the time.

SOLBERG #16—1991above
2013—below

SOLBERG #16—1991above
2014—below

View of the city of Charlotte Amalie and Hassel
Island from the South Balcony of Solberg#16

How in God's heaven could the judge be doing an excellent job during the first year of his incumbency, 1951–1952, but as soon as the pillars for the new hilltop residence began to visibly sprout out of the foundation so that they could be clearly seen in the city and the news got around that yes, it was true, it was Judge Christian who was building that palace, that all of a sudden, my job performance rating did not just drop or plummet but collapsed? Not only was I not doing an excellent job, a good job, a fair job, but I was definitely doing a terrible job. I had not become sick, demented, had been performing just as before, if anything with more experience and expertise. Just a coincidence or accident? Perhaps.

But I went on after my removal from office to finish the house and to build No. 36 Agnes Fancy, No. 1 Regjerrings Gade, and No. 38 Solberg for my beloved stepdaughter, Reubina, to occupy.

The moral of my housing experience in the Virgin Islands has to be: One should try to make every cross in his life a stepping stone instead of a tombstone.

CHAPTER XV

Why I Wished so Hard to Give My Children the Best Education Possible

One of the first things I learned about education was the tradition—a sacred tenet among the native population if you will—that the boy child was entitled to go to school only until he attained the age of thirteen (13) years. After that, he must leave school and go to work. Nothing was said about the girl child. I suppose she did not even have the right to remain that long in school or to go there at all to get an education.

But that old sage—my maternal grandfather, Alexander Benjamin—told me one of his many instructive stories one day, which gave me some enlightenment as to the reason for this rule. It showed clearly that the rule applied only to the boy child of the Blacks and was a part of the socioeconomic structure and mores of the time to build up and preserve a particular class system, one in which the White man would forever be assured a societally built-in, although personally unearned and unmerited, advantage and position of superiority over all the rest of his society.

The old man told me that if you looked at the Black man's child, compared him with the White man's child, you would at first face quickly and inevitably come to the conclusion that the White man's son is innately superior to the Black man's son.

But he continued, "Do not be fooled by this first and apparently reasonable appearance—Not so at all." The true reason for the almost-universal apparent superiority of the White boy over the Black boy is that the White one—from before his birth, while he is in the womb, immediately after his birth, through infancy, throughout his childhood, his adolescence, and even after—is given the best social conditions and the best education he is capable of receiving and obtains all aid and assistance he needs, including steadfast attention to his physical health, nurture, and educational needs. Whereas the Black child is to that same degree, both prepartum and postpartum, deprived of all the aid and assistance he needs to compete on a fair and equal basis.

The parents of the one boy have a comfortable, secure house. The parents of the other usually live in a rat-infested hovel that is rarely any better than a torture chamber. Good nutrition and medical care are enjoyed throughout the period of gestation by the mother of the White boy. The opposite is true of the Black boy's mother. Acceptable postpartum care is dispensed to the mother of the White boy, both for her health and general well-being and that of her child. Neglect of infant defects and high mortality are the order of the day for the Black mother and her child. The White child gets the best tutors at home and out of the home, both public and private. When the White child exhausts the available levels of education in his native land, if he wants it, he is promptly shipped out to wherever the desire leads—the West Indies, America, Canada, and Europe—to continue his education. And when the White child returns home armed with that excellent biological, educational, physical, mental, and emotionally solid beginning, if he needs it, he's given the amount of capital necessary to set him up in his chosen calling or profession. But the Black boy must stop school as he attains the age of thirteen (13) years, no matter how intellectually gifted he might be. And the Black girl may very well have been taken out of school long before even that, if indeed she was permitted to even begin, with its obvious inescapable results on her entire future in the society of the day.

Now the old man asked me, "Is it the race or color of the skin that really makes the difference, or the aid and assistance or lack of it that lay at the bottom of the usually vast obvious and disturbing difference between the levels of personal development of the two men's sons?"

Aggravating the situation was my own experience with my very own father. He was innately a very bright and gifted man but a staunch devotee and follower of the traditions and mores of the time. He had a great relationship with many of the buckras (White masters) of the time. He was the master carpenter who designed, built, and repaired the great houses and other buildings in which they resided in splendor and trained numerous apprentices to assist him in the work. And he believed in these masters, in their principles, and in the status quo. No matter how the relative innate gifts or talents of their sons compared with the innate gifts or talents of his sons, their sons should be beneficiaries of unlimited aid and assistance to achieve the highest potential of their personal development, but his sons must quit school at thirteen (13). That was the inexorable orthodoxy of that day and time.

Well, I happened to head my classes from first through the tenth grade. And so with the strong urging of the Belgian Sisters and because of the many praises and encomiums my father was getting every year when cards were given out, he either forgot I had reached thirteen (13) or looked the other way until I graduated in 1933 at sixteen (16) as the valedictorian of the class.

But that would be it! When the sisters, the priests, relatives, and friends dared to suggest that I be allowed to continue my education, he exploded and let it be known that at that very hour and time, lawyers and doctors were walking the streets of New York starving. Why add another educated pauper to this long hapless list? Of course, forgotten in the torrent of objections was the fact that what the members of the cloth were advocating was that I be sent to study for the Catholic priesthood, not medicine or the law. When this fact was pointed out, my father was not to be outdone. "Not my son. They won't tuck him away in some remote corner of Africa." Who could argue against that judgment? But was that the real reason for not allowing me to continue my education, or was it the same old tradition—the native Black must get only so much education and no more? And should I not be grateful that I was allowed, albeit grudgingly, to continue for an extra three years?

Well, as I grew up, I became more and more convinced of the true picture and the sinister, vicious, selfish, greedy reasons for it—of the crass injustice of it all. And the more I thought of it, the more angry I became. And the more angry I became, the more determined I became that I would give myself the best education I could with whatever resources I had. Secondly, that my Black children would be given nothing less than the best any White child received in upbringing—from before conception, during gestation, after birth, in childhood, adolescence, and even after the formal educational years were spent, if necessary, to become established in their chosen fields for their life's work. No child, White or Black, would have a better chance to survive and compete, if only the child had what it takes, and would let me help.

My reward for that resolution and steadfast dedication has been great.

When I was named Judge of the Police Court of Saint Thomas and Saint John eighteen (18) years after my graduation in 1933 (two years after my admission to the Bar of the Virgin Islands at age thirty-four [34]) and the news reached my father in Frederiksted, I was told by my mother that he wept like a baby for joy and maybe because of remorse of conscience because it wasn't that he couldn't but wouldn't help. He allowed himself and his children, notwithstanding the great talent he was, to be victimized by a rather rotten and corrupt tradition borne of and nurtured by prejudice, selfishness, and greed.

And each and all the six children I raised, both of the half blood and the whole blood—Reubina, Alicia, Delano, Barbara, Alphonso II, and Cora—have given excellent acquaintances and full satisfaction for the patrimony expended on them thus far for their physical, mental, educational, emotional, and spiritual development and advancement.

From the balcony of #16 Solberg—Barbara,
Dad, Mom, Alphonso II, Cora

With the help of the Almighty and of my dear wife (Ruth) and some great benefactors (i.e., Ralph Paiewonsky, Herman E. Moore, Omar Brown), I broke that awful, terrible tradition—a veritable yoke around the neck of the Black man's son.

The above entrenched tradition is not reported here to create or foster dislike or malice for any person or class. Nor is it my intention that any person of color should use it as a justification or as a perennial excuse for failing to use to the utmost the many advantages and opportunities existing today for self-improvement and progress. I relate it only as one of the very significant annals in the history of the Virgin Islands and probably of the Caribbean.

Reubina

Delano

Alicia

CHAPTER XVI

My Experiences in Public Life

I held several minor positions in public life following my departure from A. H. Lockhart & Co., and from the Firm of A. H. Riise in both of which I worked as stenographer and assistant bookkeeper. These included brief periods in the Police Department through the kindness of Adolph Gereau, its Chief Clerk; the Department of Public Works when jolly, burly, able, and very witty Donald S. Boreham (Uncle Donald) was superintendent; as secretary to the committee in charge of the local celebration of the sesquicentennial year of the adoption of the Constitution of the United States under the able chairmanship of Honorable Conrad Corneiro, then chairman of the Municipal Council of Saint Thomas and Saint John—the local legislative body; and as part-time stenographer during the sessions of the Municipal Council.

But it was in 1941 that I received my first meaningful appointment to a position of public service. Beginning as clerk stenographer to the Municipal Council of Saint Thomas and Saint John and the Legislative Assembly of the Virgin Islands—which was constituted by the Municipal Council of Saint Thomas and Saint John and the Municipal Council of Saint Croix, meeting at least once a year in joint session in the capital island of Saint Thomas—I moved to Chief Clerk and then Executive Secretary of the Body on the retirement within a year of my first appointment of the then Executive Secretary, the kind and amiable Benito Smith.

As Executive Secretary, I was charged with the duties of monitoring and answering all incoming correspondence; keeping an eye on the progress of legislation whether it originated in the body or from the Governor's Office; attending committee meetings, especially those of the Committee of the Whole; taking verbatim and transcribing the minutes of the proceedings of the Council when in formal session; and generally overseeing the orderly, efficient, and businesslike operation and functioning of the office of the Legislature.

In discharging these duties, I soon found myself in the middle of two factions or blocs into which the seven-member body had split. One of these blocs was dead set against me and so would have fired me instantly if only it could, and the other was just as resolutely in my favor and for my continuation in office. This division occurred although all the members of both blocs had all come from one and the same party. But having routed and silenced, for the time being anyway, all outside opposition, the battle-tested and hungry troops had to find somebody to do battle with. And where else could these be found but within the ranks of the party itself? Thank God, the faction on my side was the majority one and that it never wavered in its support. If it did, I am certain my career as a public servant of some account would have ended almost before it really got off the ground. While the particular members of this bare majority changed in some degree from election to election, it held fast as the majority bloc. And I will ever be grateful to the Honorable Omar Brown, Ralph Paiewonsky, Julius Sprauve, Osmond Kean, and Harry deLagarde for their support when it counted most.

In those days, the Legislature seldom met in formal session in the daytime, usually only to consider emergency matters. It was believed that a great political plus was achieved by having these sessions at night so that the mainstream of the constituencies of the elected members, most of whom worked in the daytime, could come and see their representatives hard at work on their behalf, usually from 8:30 p.m. Some sessions lasted well after midnight, and believe it or not, there was only one office staff for both day and night work. It was not unusual for those employees to put in twelve (12)- to sixteen (16)-hour days *without complaint*. That's the way it was.

After passing the Virgin Islands Bar in 1949, the legislature rewarded my past service of eight years with a promotion from executive secretary of the legislature to the newly created office of legal aide to the body with a substantial increase in pay. Now enjoying the imprimatur and prestige of the legal profession and the authority of functioning as an attorney at law in the Islands, the Legislature charged me with the responsibility of sitting in meetings and giving my legal opinion on pending legislation and drafting and amending more pending legislation than formerly. I could now also give much more meaningful aid and speak with more legal authority to many of the constituents of the several councilmen, which might well result in a political plus for them.

Swearing in ceremony as Judge of the Police Court 1951 L to R: Governor Morris F. deCastro, Alphonso A Christian I, Judge Herman E. Moore

After serving two years in the position of legal aid to the legislature, Judge Carl G. Thiele—of the Police Court of Saint Thomas and

Saint John—died. You will recall the details I previously reported, which followed how—sparked by a campaign of the Council led by Omar Brown, fresh from a West Indian Conference in Barbados—I eventually was appointed and confirmed to be Judge of the Police Court of Saint Thomas and Saint John in August of 1951.

I enjoyed working in this position, although I had to serve at the same time as coroner, recorder of deeds, and chairman of the Board of Elections and although—perhaps due to efforts of mine at self-improvement (I began building my home on the hill and bought a new car)—I did not enjoy a friendly press for about the last two years of my three-year incumbency. This position was truly the first great responsibility I bore as a public servant with ultimate responsibility and accountability for the functioning of a department of government. And while it was the cause and source of many unpleasant and even agonizing moments on balance, I must say it also became and served as the rich source, in fact the fountainhead, of many achievements realized and enjoyed both during and after the time I held that office.

From October 1, 1954 (when my first term as Judge ended), to November 1972 (when I was appointed Commissioner of Public Safety for the Virgin Islands), I practiced law exclusively as a general practitioner. I am told that Governor Melvin H. Evans, who appointed me, did so at the urging of the more staid, conservative, substantial, and to some extent, scared inhabitants of the Territory.

L to R: Atty John Maduro, Gov. Melvin Evans,
Judge Alphonso Christian, Judge Almeric Christian
Appointment of Judge Alphonso A. Christian
I as Commissioner of Public Safety

It must be remembered that the appointment, which came in November 1972, was only months after the brutal murders at Fountain Valley and Bruau House in Saint Croix, which occurred in quick succession. The community as a whole was in the depths of shock, melancholia, and fear. I also understand that several other outstanding persons had been offered the position and had turned it down. When I informed my wife that it had been offered to me, she was instantly and vociferously opposed. It took days of reasoning and strong importunities for her to moderate and then neutralize and finally change her position.

The appointment, which followed, received the blessings of the press, the community, and the unanimous confirmation of the legislature.

We would begin to attempt to restore an appreciable degree of faith in the citizenry that the Islands had not been suddenly transformed into a haven for criminals where the law-abiding were not safe and from which they would do well to depart posthaste. To accomplish this, we would have to rebuild the police force, increase security and understanding at the prisons, and take the necessary steps to reduce substantially the risk of unfriendly fires. For at that time, the department oversaw not only the police but also the Bureau of Corrections and the Fire Division. Besides these three divisions— Police, Corrections, Fire—the department listed as its fourth division, the administrative division.

If we were to make any headway at all, it was imperative that we reduce fighting and skirmishes within our own house to a minimum. Each of the four divisions of the department was given the benefit of a plenary (gripe) session with the commissioner once a month when every officer or employee was privileged to unburden himself of all that interfered with the efficient and enjoyable performance of his duties whether justified or not. In cases where particular problems proved too serious or time-consuming for the time available in a given session, these cases were laid aside for the special consideration they required at a later time with the commissioner personally in his office. Additionally, where issues or problems arose between sessions that would or could not wait, every officer and employee had a standing invitation to make an appointment with the office of the commissioner for a special private audience.

Ruth, his wife, pinning Commissioner Alphonso Christian
I as the new Commissioner of Public Safety, 1972

Our chief objective had perforce to be not public posturing but quiet and private real, substantial official achievement and progress. Indeed, I cannot remember one instance in which we had any public exposé that should and could have been handled in-house, unlike the present, thanks probably to the current proliferation of radio talk shows, some of which do have undeniable merit.

The rewards were obvious and truly gratifying to all the men. Men of all ranks within each division and between divisions moved closer to each other; the esprit de corps grew; and with the increased unity and cohesiveness, our achievements in a very difficult period in the history of the department were at least respectable.

There are those who clamored for my removal in 1974 on the election of Governor Cyril E. King, who succeeded Governor Melvin H. Evans, who it will be remembered appointed me in 1972, partly because of party politics and partly because some were disappointed that we did not succeed in changing the immanently iniquitous nature of man and wiping out crime entirely from the Virgin Islands. Since we could never hope to entirely abolish either political considerations in the operation of government created by the votes of the general populace or to change the inherently sinful nature of man, we were not too unhappy with these philosophically misguided and unhappy souls, who clearly were totally unmindful of the realities and the vicissitudes of this life. In fact, when my successor, Dr. Winston Gibson, was appointed, I felt Governor King had done me a great favor. I only realized how big a favor it was when (as the months passed) I truly came to grips with the incredible degree of deterioration and decay my properties (real and personal) and my personal affairs generally were suffering due to my total absorption into and with the position of commissioner from 1972 to 1975.

I set to work, putting my private house in order in October of 1975 after the most grueling and demanding and exhausting public office I had held so far. I also returned to the practice of the law on a more regular basis, half day, from early 1976 and continued until April 1978, with the able clerical assistance of Mr. Earle Francis.

In or about November of 1977, the Honorable Verne A. Hodge, Chief Judge of the Territorial Court, wrote me the following letter:

> Dear Judge Christian:
>
> Enclosed for your information is a copy of Act No. 4053 pertaining to the utilization of former Municipal Court Judges as Senior Sitting Judges in the Territorial Court.
>
> As you may know the workload of the new Territorial Court is such that your service as a Senior Sitting Judge is needed, even on a part time basis, if we are to maintain an acceptable level of judicial services to the people of the Virgin Islands. Accordingly, any assistance that you may be able to render will be greatly appreciated, and I shall be available at your convenience to discuss the matter with you in more detail. If you are available to assist us, please call me or

Mrs. Viola Smith, so that we may arrange such a meeting.

Sincerely,
/s/ Verne A. Hodge
Presiding Judge

I accepted this position on contract and began discharging the duties of this office as the first senior sitting judge under the new act on April 14, 1978.

To give me some modern pointers, briefing, and instruction on probate law, which I would be chiefly concerned with, I was sent to attend a course given for probate judges at the University of Nevada for two weeks. On my return, I would have the full jurisdiction of any other judge of the Territorial Court, but I would chiefly be occupied with the timely processing of all probate cases and presiding in probable cause and advice of rights hearings, conciliation hearings, civil restraint hearings, and marriage ceremonies.

Within about two years, this step taken by Judge Hodge had resulted in basically making uniform the procedures followed in our Court in the administration of the estates of deceased persons, now adjudicated mainly by one (instead of three) judge, each with his or her view of what both the substantive and adjective or procedural law and rules were on the subject—completely eliminating the large existing backlog and expediting the processing of newly filed probate cases. As a result, the judge saw no difficulty to be encountered in adding to my assignments presiding in sessions dealing with small claims, traffic, and support cases, as well as an occasional case of partition, injunction, damages for negligence, divorce, or paternity case, or other civil as well as criminal cases.

As I write this chapter in these Memoirs, I am serving in the fourth year of my fifth public office and I believe I have truly kept faith with what I said when I was sworn in as a senior sitting judge on May 10, 1978.

For years, even while probate administration lay exclusively in the jurisdiction of the District Court, this area of judicial work was treated as a stepchild in relation to all the many other subjects of judicial work. This was so particularly with respect to attorneys but even so to some extent by some judges. Probate cases would be taken off the back burner of all legal work *only* if there were no other class of cases pending, and this was seldom if ever true. Thus, the administration of the estates of deceased persons, like them, reposed as it were, in a veritable graveyard.

In receiving jurisdiction of this legal and judicial stepchild, the present administration of the Court, led by Chief Judge Hodge, intends to change all that. He has assigned me the task of following through on this long-overdue initiative taken by him and the Court. And I intend to discharge this function with dedication, vigor, and to the best of my ability. In performing this assignment, I intend to carry out the legislative intent of the Senate as approved by the Governor. I will do all I can to fulfill the clear purpose of the Chief Judge in selecting me for this role; all the lawyers can be assured of my fullest cooperation; and above all, the heirs and next of kin of the estates can rest confident that they now have a court that will assiduously look after their best interest, not only in seeing to it that they receive the share of the estate of their ancestors to which they are legally entitled but that they receive it and thus be able to enjoy it in the shortest possible time permitted by law.

If my work as a civil servant has embedded one principle firmly in me, it is this: That in every position I had held, I have always wanted to serve with great zeal and thoroughness; I have learned considerably from each incumbency; and after I left, I always felt a true sense of relief, inner fulfillment, and satisfaction.

CHAPTER XVII

My Periods of Intense Agony
in the Practice of the Law

It is said that in every worthwhile undertaking, in every life's work (indeed in every life), there are crosses to bear and that the really important factor in this is not the crosses themselves (though difficult they might be) but the attitude, the approach, and the disposition of the crossbearer in relation to the problems with which he or she is confronted.

Sometimes these crosses are unrelated to one's fellowmen, not at all of their making—such as illness, personal injury from accident, loss, or substantial reduction of employment due to community-wide economic circumstances as periodically obtain in recessionary periods in which our country or territory finds itself. At other times, these reverses one suffers are the result and outgrowth of the vicious and malicious plotting of one's very own fellowmen, at times members of his own calling, even of his own family. Since I am involved—am the one upon whom these crosses were leveled and who was forced to bear them—I shall make an honest effort to just state the facts and leave it to the reader to draw his own conclusion as to the true cause and source and merit of these agonizing experiences through which I had to live in the first fifteen (15) years of my practice of the law.

There is a local concept that whenever one has a period of great success and rejoicing, a Palm Sunday if you will, there is sure to follow his Good Friday. Some individual or group is sure to see to that. Well, my Palm Sunday might be said to have consisted of the passing of the Bar of both the Courts of the Virgin Islands and the Court of Appeals for the Third Circuit; my immediate promotion as a result thereof from Executive Secretary to the Legislature to Legal Aid to the Legislature with the almost doubling of my pay; an instant abundant legal clientele, which resulted from my being so widely known due to my long membership in and my emceeing of the recent biennial political campaigns of the VI Progressive Guide for election of members of the local Legislature; the increased income, which I earned from these undertakings; my investiture as Police Judge at the relatively young age of thirty-four (34); my building of a very noticeable residence on Estate Solberg hill; and the fact that, notwithstanding my removal from the Bench in 1954, I continued to attract as much as half of the cases of the then Municipal Court and even on the docket of the District Court at times.

Removing me from the Judgeship of the Police Court was supposed to accomplish at once three adverse effects with one blow. I would lose the honor of a sitting judge. Secondly, I was regarded as a strict or stern judge, so I would not only lose my salary as a paid official of the Government but even if I went into the private practice of law, hardly anyone would patronize me. Thirdly, I would not only lose my prestige as Judge and my income, but I would lose the mansion on the hill—no prestige or income, no money to finish the house.

But a local saying is that God is high but looks low. It quickly became clear that neither the plot nor the plotters got His blessing. The ultimate goal of the conspiracy was a complete failure. The people flocked into my little office diagonally across from the now Enid M. Baa Library over the gut, No. 4 Guttets Gade. My real problem was not enough clients but how to find the time, the know-how, and the energy to serve them properly and faithfully. My income, instead of being wiped out, increased substantially. I could still support my family, educate the children in prestigious schools, and pay for the house in less time than had been originally expected.

So vicious plot number one to destroy me having failed, do we throw in the sponge or make at least one more try? Yes, that is what we will do. But precisely what? Charge him with a crime as they did

Omar Brown twelve (12) years earlier? No, that probably won't work. What, with the right of trial by jury? And besides, Judge Moore is still on the Bench and he would never stand for any glaring injustice against anyone. Besides, we believe he likes Alphonso Christian. Christian appears to be one of his fair-headed boys.

As I mention Judge Moore, I believe he must have been approached with this second plot because what else could evoke the spontaneous exclamation from that honorable gentleman while I was trying a case before him one day to the effect that "just can't stop Judge Christian from practicing law." Recalling this experience many years later, as plot number two unfolded with Judge Walter M. Gordon presiding as Judge Moore's immediate successor, I can't but conclude that an attempt was made to use Judge Moore for the implementation of the plot, but he—at least passively if not affirmatively—declined. But since we had a new administration in Washington (the Eisenhower Republican Administration) and now in 1956–1957, Judge Moore (a Democrat) just will not be reappointed, we can wait for the investiture of the new judge, who has no true knowledge of who Alphonso Christian or any other longtime inhabitant of the Virgin Islands is and might care less about doing gross injustice to any such and then we will carefully concoct and move plot two along. This time, we must not fail.

But what was plot number two as it unfolded? We will not charge him with a crime, for then he has the whole panoply of legal protections and safeguards of the Bill of Rights as enshrined in the Constitution of the United States and the 1954 Revised Organic Act of the Virgin Islands—right to counsel, trial by jury of his peers, and all that nonsense. If all those veritable obstacles are involved, we just can't be certain of success. And this time around, we must not fail. So let's charge him with violation of the Code of Legal Ethics, for the trier of the fact(s) here is no jury but our very own Judge Gordon. If we have him on our side, we just can't lose.

In addition to being a local Black boy who was succeeding in the practice of the law, although he never attended intramural college, I had had the misfortune in the past of talking up to Attorney William Cox in the parking lot next to the Emancipation Garden, which I learned later was the most terrible thing to do—a thing to which he was totally unaccustomed in the part of the country from which he came. I had also had the misfortune of not cowing 100 percent to what I considered less-than-acceptable judicial rulings in a case in which I defended a poor defendant charged with voluntary manslaughter tried before Judge Gordon, who appeared to be Attorney Cox's close buddy and friend. In fact, the experience of many lawyers at the time was if they were unfortunate enough to appear before Gordon with Cox on the other side, they could forget it, unless one or two very exceptional circumstances also coexisted.

Well, in 1958, Judge Gordon was sworn in as Judge of the District Court, succeeding Judge Herman E. Moore. Within a little more than one year, I was charged with violating the Code of Legal Ethics. In addition to Judge Gordon (who judged the case), Attorney David Maas (Chairman of the Grievance Committee) prosecuted. All three (Cox, Gordon, and Maas) were powerful Republicans. The press was fed with frequent, if not daily, releases of the inherently dishonest, dishonorable, and unethical nature of this case. This they did for nearly two years before a Judgment of guilty was entered.

The sentence for albeit such a grievous assault on the sacred code? A reprimand. Regardless of the enormity and perhaps overabundance of legal errors in the proceeding and the apparent injustice, who would appeal where the sentence is only a reprimand? Moreover, locally, Judge Gordon was then the sole head of the judiciary, for at the time, we had only one Federal District Judge, not two as later developed. Let's keep it local. If there was an appeal, no one knew what the judges of the Court of Appeals for the Third Circuit (who were only too aware of Gordon's track record) would think.

But what was the transaction out of which the charge arose? One of my long-term clients was a lady named Lucille Sewer, a childless merchant of many years, who knew me from the early days when I began working for the firm of A. H. Lockhart in 1934. She had raised five foster children. When she was afflicted with what turned out to be her last illness, she called me to her home to make her will. When I arrived there, she was in no mood, even if she was in condition to proceed, and so she told me to return some other time. The next day,

I was called to the hospital where she had been taken to assist her in making her will. I asked her doctor if he believed she had the mental capacity to make a will to which he said no, and I left the hospital. On the following morning, Miss Lillian Mills, sister and only heir at law apparent of Lucille Sewer, came to my office with some of the foster children raised by her sister and told me she was very disappointed that her sick sister could not make a will because she knew her sister's intention was to give whatever her net estate was to the five foster children raised by her as she liked them as if they were her own children. She raised them, and whatever she had, they helped her acquire it. Miss Mills therefore said she, too, wanted the children to get the estate that she would inherit if her sister died without a will. She, therefore, asked me to put that in writing, which I did as follows:

Agreement Transferring Property
as Heir Apparent

KNOW ALL MEN BY THESE PRESENTS:

That, for and in consideration of the sum of $1.00 (One Dollar), U.S. Currency, and for other good and valuable considerations, the receipt where-of is hereby acknowledged, I, LILLIAN MILLS, a single woman, of St. Thomas, Virgin Islands, on this 19th day of May, A.D., 1958, at St. Thomas, Virgin Islands, hereby agree to convey, grant and transfer, and by these presents do convey, grant and transfer unto Warren Hendricks, Theophilus Larson, and Edith Thomas, all residents of St. Thomas, Virgin Islands; and to Dorothy Sewer Birch and Liston Sewer, both residents of New York, N.Y., share and share alike, all such property, real and personal and mixed, wherever situated, as I may inherit or come into possession or ownership of as heir at law or testamentary heir from my sister, LUCILLE MILLS SEWER, of St. Thomas, Virgin Islands, now seriously ill and hospitalized at the Knud Hansen Memorial Hospital.

A IN WITNESS WHEREOF, I have hereunto subscribed my name and affixed my Seal this 19th day of May, A.D., 1958, at Charlotte Amalie, St. Thomas, Virgin Islands.

/s/ Lillian Mills
Lillian Mills (Seal)
Signed, sealed and delivered
in the presence of:

/s/ Alphonso A. Christian
/s/ Barbara T. Christian
/s/ Helen Jarvis

TERRITORY OF THE VIRGIN ISLANDS)

District of St. Thomas) ss: Acknowledgment

BE IT REMEMBERED that on this 19th day of May, A.D., 1958, before me personally appeared LILLIAN MILLS, to me personally known and known to me to be the person who executed the foregoing instrument, and after explaining to her the full import and effect of the said instrument, she did acknowledge that she executed the same freely and voluntarily for the purposes therein stated.

A/s/ G. de Castro
NOTARY PUBLIC

Sometime later, after Lucille Sewer's death, I instituted a probate proceeding to have the net estate of the deceased transferred on the record to the five children she raised as they appeared in the above document as Miss Mills had told me was the wish and intent of both her deceased sister and herself.

Attorney John Maduro, who was just then beginning to practice, was retained by Miss Lillian Mills to have the document drawn by me canceled and the property left by Lucille Sewer transferred to Lillian Mills instead of the five foster children of the deceased on the ground that she did not understand what she had done when she signed the transfer—although she initiated it, asked me to put it in writing, and the writing was explained to her both by me and by a notary in the presence of three witnesses.

I, therefore, refused to admit that I had done anything wrong in drawing the instrument in question.

However, here was opportunity number one to discredit me. The Court would find all the facts against me in the suit to cancel the document, it would give the property to Miss Mills, and what is more, a case would be instituted against me on the court's initiative—the same court that would try the case for violation of several of the canons of legal ethics.

I do not fault Attorney Maduro for his part in the plan. After all, he was only doing his job as an advocate and to build his young fledgling practice. Moreover, what probably did not enter his mind was the fact that if I had been disbarred, about 50 percent of the people who constituted my clientele were excellent potential clients of his. One person whose identity I really do not remember even allowed that when she told Mr. Maduro a position I held on the law in a pending case during this murky period, he remarked, "Don't worry about it—what Attorney Christian thinks. He will be disbarred." But we all know how some folks try to stir up as much trouble and enmity as they can. So I give little attention and no credence to this story. Besides, who could fault a young attorney for cooperating with such an awesome combine, which appeared to have the blessing of the very powerful Judge of the District Court? You have to at the very least admit that the temptation was considerable, maybe irresistible.

The adverse publicity, which was generated by this case, lasted continuously for about three years. But in 1960, when the publicity appeared to be taking its toll, a most ironic and surprising thing happened. I later regarded it as a miracle. This was a general election year. The Unity Democratic Party had been in power continuously ever since the election of President Eisenhower (a republican) in 1952, and before (to the endless chagrin of the local Republican Party) and the Republican Party wanted to make a last-ditch effort to establish even a small semblance of a two-party system in the Islands. This they resolved to do in formal session assembled. Instrumental in the leadership of the party at this time were Omar Brown, Chairman; Carlos A. Downing; and Roy P. Gordon. The Party, led by these three men with whom I worked very closely in both the VI Progressive Guide and the Legislature, decided it will try to achieve its objective by running two candidates at large—one White, one Black. At this very time that a top all-Republican combine of the judiciary and Bar of which I was a part (Judge Gordon, Bill Cox, Dave Maas) was embarked on what appeared to me to be a well-thought-out plot to discredit and disbar me and if possible, reduce me to a state of public disgrace, penury, and want, the local Republican Party to which the Combine at least apparently belong was nominating me by acclamation to run with Mrs. Ethel Byers at large as the party's two standard bearers for 1960 to be members of the Legislature.

This development at once accomplished many obvious results, which prompted Attorney Maas (the preferer of the charges) to remark to Chairman Omar Brown (whom Maas had successfully defended fourteen (14) years earlier when Omar was charged with a criminal offense): "You certainly made a mess of things, saddling us with Alphonso Christian at this crucial time," or words to that effect.

The first effect was to drain the Bar's position of all credibility, especially as Gordon was identified with the prosecutors or persecutors or harassers (whichever term you prefer) and he had not been too much of a public favorite either as Governor or Judge. Secondly, it gave me a beautiful and impregnable forum for telling in public my side of the case, as now I was not just an attorney but a candidate for public office, not self-appointed but elected by acclamation of the prestigious Republican Party, the party of the same prestigious Combine working against me. Thirdly, the public is made aware of the true objective of the Combine and that Judge Gordon was anything but impartial in the case in which he was sitting as judge against Attorney Christian and did not like Attorney Christian. Therefore, while they gave me only those matters in the District Court in which Judge Gordon had little or no say—such as debt, uncontested divorce, change of name, custody, bankruptcy, and probate cases—they made up for the loss by substantially increasing the cases they brought to me in other forums, such as the Municipal Court and various quasi-judicial bodies. The bottom line was that my income hardly suffered. In fact, more Republicans, notwithstanding all the daily adverse publicity in the media, brought me substantial business I never got before because I was now one of them, one of their legislative candidates. In fact, I remember well one prominent Republican remarking to me after studying the facts: "They charged you with unethical conduct. They are guilty of larceny. Who do they refer to? I do not know."

The irony of this story is that the party fielded and ran me as one of their candidates, although I was never a registered republican. That is why I truly believe God had a big hand in this whole sordid affair.

These three years was a time of great suffering for me. The crosses seemed not unbearable but incredible. How could your fellow human beings be so vicious? If I had done these people any harm, the lengths to which they went would be understandable if not excusable. But I learned two great lessons from all this. First, it is not easy to fool the people in the long run. Given a reasonable time, they will put their finger on the true facts, the true villains. Secondly, never give up when your time comes to suffer. Just pray to God and have faith. Even when you suffer alone, with no relative or friend who understands or stands by you, continue to pray and to have faith and you will not only survive but be stronger and wiser because of your suffering, your prayers, your faith, and your perseverance. So it was with me in this first bout with the Bar and Judge Gordon.

By now, I believed I was out of the woods, but I was wrong. I am in for cross case number two. This lasted for two more years, from 1961 to 1963. As I feverishly prepared to leave for a much-needed annual vacation to the States, a client of mine anxiously came to the office and informed me her husband had just been charged with rape in the first degree and she wanted to retain me to represent him. I declined due to my imminent departure from the Islands. I remained for a month. And on my return, the lady anxiously returned to my office and informed me that she had given the case to Attorney Croxton Williams in my absence, but now that I was back, she would like me to take over from this point on. I checked with Attorney Williams, and the change of counsel was amicably arranged.

A plea of not guilty had been entered and a jury trial demanded. In those days, when a jury trial was to take place, the practice was to give to attorneys for both the prosecution and the defendant(s) copies of the general panel, usually containing about sixty (60) names, from which the trial panel would be chosen. The reason was so counsel could examine the names on the panel with his client and any other helpful persons at his disposal to adequately prepare for the voir dire examination and the making of challenges for cause. These are challenges against particular persons drawn to serve and seeking their removal from the trial panel on the grounds that for any one or more of a multitude of acceptable legal reasons, they will not or cannot deal fairly and impartially with either side of the case whether the government or the defendant(s).

When I got my copy of the list of potential jurors, I immediately called in the defendant's wife and being occupied with a host of other matters, entrusted it to her to take it home, study the names on it, and if she objected to any of them, to let me know in the next day or two with the reasons for her objections.

What the lady did with the list showed that she loved her husband very dearly. She not only studied the list for appropriate legal challenges for cause but contacted a number of persons whose names appeared thereon and asked them to give some sort of consideration to her husband—not necessarily to go against the evidence but not to go too hard with him. At least that was what she told me.

I replied to her that on the voir dire examination, the jurors will be asked appropriate questions as a result of which they will inform the court the nature and extent of these contacts and their effect on the ability of the jurors, taking them into due consideration, to nevertheless render a fair and impartial verdict based only on the evidence adduced at the trial.

When the day of trial came, on the customary examination, the jurors contacted stated what took place regarding the defendant's wife contacting them on the case. Judge Gordon asked me if the defendant's wife had informed me to that effect, to which I answered in the affirmative. He then wanted to know why I did not immediately contact the Court and advise the Court to the effect, to which I replied exactly what I told the defendant's wife—that I was sure, on voir dire, the jurors would reveal the nature and extent of the matter in each case and the court would then make the appropriate decision with or without the benefit of challenges for cause whether or not the jurors could be relied upon to render a fair and impartial verdict based only on the evidence presented at the trial.

But Judge Gordon, after discussing the matter with the special committee, was persuaded that I should be tried and punished for unethical conduct in that by not immediately unilaterally bringing the matter to him in chambers but electing to wait until it was revealed on voir dire, I had aided the wife of the defendant in an attempt at jury tampering. And the second ordeal was on with all the almost-daily releases in the press, which could not but tend to drive home the fact that, surely, something must be wrong in Denmark.

And it seemed they were indeed achieving this goal handsomely from some of the comments I heard from some of my dearest friends. It was felt when the term jury tampering had been aired and used, for all it implied (long enough) that surely, this most serious case (following so close in tandem right on the very heels of the prior case) might very likely (or should) result in my disbarment. When I explained to one of my girlfriends what this meant, she replied, "Yes, Alphonso, I think it would be best for you to stop practicing, at least for a while." My dearest male friend who visited my law office almost every day (God bless his soul) allowed that (after all) he, too, was convinced from the lengthy, disparaging barrage that my girlfriend was probably on the right track. Even my most influential, sincere, and respected friend, Judge Moore, told me words to the effect that it appeared that I was becoming problem prone.

Add to the probable effect of the above on my spiritual, mental, and emotional health the many tense steps through which I was taken by the powers that be. There was the examination under oath by the bar grievance committee headed by our good friend David Maas. He was still the man to build the case for an adverse committee vote and in preparation and to lay the groundwork for the trial by the judge of the case for disciplining the attorney. Cox was ready to prosecute in court as soon as the adverse finding and recommendation for trial (the equivalent of an indictment or information in formal criminal proceedings) was returned. And the third and final person in the stairway to the objective, the Honorable Judge Gordon (who instituted the proceedings in the first instance by referring it to his fellow republicans for action), was ready, willing, and able to do his job to preside at my trial.

In the meantime, the media was more diligent than ever in creating the right public state of mind to accept what by now was clearly the predictable result.

I was by now more depressed. I seemed to have only one person to whom I can pour out my soul and I made use of it. But I was still becoming increasingly unsure of my position. So while the case was in progress, I talked to my good friend (the late Cyril Michael) and asked him what he thought of my voluntarily suspending my practice, even for a limited time. His answer changed my entire spirit and outlook. He said, "Don't do any such thing. Don't let them drive you out of your hard-earned profession. When they are all gone, you will still be here." And so it was.

A second strong rebuilder of my sorely depressed spirit came from the then-serving United States attorney, the late Leon Miller. He strongly encouraged me to stay on and fight on. To underscore the sincerity of his advice, he informed me that he went through a similar experience in his home state of West Virginia and now he is serving as United States attorney of the Virgin Islands. And he added, "Judge Christian, five years from now, you will look back and you will wonder what really you were worrying so much about." And so it was.

During the trial, all the honorable men were duly assembled and played their assigned parts flawlessly, so flawlessly indeed that an old, decent, and truly honorable attorney who was still around (unlike most of the actors in the case after he had seen the entire performance) remarked, "But the judge seemed so severe!" This was the kind and beloved Daniel W. Ambrose.

Well, after the inevitable predictable decision of guilty, the judge took the case under advisement. The sentence was suspension for six months, four months of which was suspended. Knowing what I was up against, I did not appeal but spent the time I was forbidden to practice preparing a part of my own property in the Market Square into which to remove my office from No. 4 Guttets Gade, which I had rented for many years. Also, I paid a visit to Judge Gordon and let him know I did not intend to appeal but to abide fully and completely by the terms of his Judgment.

Two years after my suspension, in 1965, I began a three-year stint as Chairman of the Virgin Islands Carnival as a public service, extracurricular activity. During the height of my first year as chairman, I received a call from Judge Gordon to visit him in his chambers. I began wondering, *Lord, what did I do this time?* As I slowly, pensively, but above all, most apprehensively entered his chambers, he called out, "Alphonso, come in. Do you mean I have to send you a special invitation for you to visit me?" So with such warm words spoken in even warmer tones, I mustered the courage to sit down with some ease, although still with some trepidation.

The judge then told me the reason for his invitation. It was the rule and practice that each federal judge, in addition to personally attending the annual judicial conference of his circuit, to appoint a member of the bar of his district as his representative at the conference. For the seven years Judge Gordon had served in the Virgin Islands thus far, he had always appointed his friend (and my prosecutor), Attorney William Cox, but he thought that the time had come when I merited the honor and should have that experience and to succeed Mr. Cox. If I would accept the appointment, he wanted me to take my wife along and make a good impression at the various sessions of the prestigious conference and at the closing banquet of the judicial conference for the Third Circuit. Well, I am sure I do not surprise anyone when I say you could have knocked me down with a feather. And the judge appointed me for the remaining three consecutive years that he spent in the Virgin Islands so that I acquired permanent-member status.

Later, I learned that William Cox had left the jurisdiction permanently. I never had the pleasure of seeing him again, and if what I heard of his whereabouts was true, I never again will.

The moral to these experiences comes from the truth of what Judge Michael and Attorney, later himself Judge, Miller advised me. Never, never, never give up fighting for your survival and personal advancement. But my attitude throughout, to this day, has been most helpful and is in accordance with Lincoln's advice: to always endeavor to fashion your actions with malice toward none. As Holy Writ put it: Judge not so that ye may not be judged. Never apply the law of retaliation. "Instead, do good to your enemies, for by so doing, you will heap coals of fire on their heads, for vengeance is mine (not any man's)," says the Lord. And is this not the basis of our man-made law that no man should take the law into his own hands—that no man has the right to dish out his own brand of justice, for if this takes place, you cannot achieve the laudable goal of equal justice under law?

Those who made might right have all vanished from the scene or at least from their pedestals, and just maybe, justice has eventually prevailed.

No less a member of that outstanding combine than Judge Walter A. Gordon closes this chapter by appointing me, whom he twice adjudged after trial as ethically unfit to be a member of the Virgin Islands Bar Association and unfit to practice in his court to represent him and the same bar in and before the prestigious Federal Third Judicial Circuit Court of Appeals.

Any reference to a plot or conspiracy or implication of any deliberate wrongdoing by any person or official who was in any way connected with either or both of these ethics cases prosecuted against me as related in these memoirs is nothing more than how the entire proceedings appeared to me. All the participants could very well have been acting in perfect good faith, doing their assigned duties and discharging the functions of their particular offices as they sincerely and honestly felt they were duty bound to do. I could have gotten the wrong impressions and arrived at the wrong conclusions. Consequently, as I said at the outset of this chapter, I leave it to each reader to objectively draw his own conclusions—totally uninfluenced by the conclusions, which I drew or intimated from the actions as they unfolded in both of these terrible crosses, which I bore in the first fifteen (15) years in the practice of my profession.

CHAPTER XVIII

The Creation of the Office of Senior Sitting Judge of the Territorial Court

The story of the creation of this office and my appointment as the first official to perform the duties of the office is such an interesting one that I am devoting this brief additional chapter to revealing just what took place. Officials who at the time were closer to the judiciary (like Judge Verne Hodge) and to the Legislature (like Senator Elmo D. Roebuck) may be able to tell it more accurately and in more detail. But this is the story as I was able to piece it together, mostly after the fact.

In 1976, during the incumbency of Governor Cyril E. King, the terms of office of the six Territorial Judges for the Territory then sitting—three in Saint Thomas and Saint John and three in Saint Croix—expired. These were Chief Judge Cyril Michael and Associate Judges Eileen Petersen and Louis Hoffman in Saint Thomas and Saint John; and Associate Judges William F. Moorehead, Antoine Joseph, and John Marsh in Saint Croix. All six aspired to reappointment, but Governor King reappointed Judges Petersen and Joseph only. The present Chief Judge, Verne A. Hodge, was appointed to succeed Judge Michael as chief judge and Henry Feuerzeig to replace Judge Hoffman. In Saint Croix, the two retired judges were replaced by Judges Raymond Finch and Irvin Silverlight.

Two lingering factors combined to sow the seed that resulted in the ultimate creation of the new office of Senior Sitting Judge of the Territorial Court of the Virgin Islands. One was the increased workload of the judges, due mainly to the transfer of jurisdiction in many areas from theDistrict Court to the Territorial Court, combined with the obvious need for as much experience as possible to supplement and if possible, complement and enhance the quality of service of so many new judicial appointments. The other was the continuing desire of the retirees, especially Judge Louis Hoffman, to serve in some capacity as judge.

So it was (I was informed) that at the persistent urging of mostly Judge Hoffman, a bill was drafted (if not by him, with much input from him) to create the new office. In fact, I was also informed that as originally drafted, only Judge Hoffman would really be eligible for appointment to this new position. From all I could gather, there is no doubt in my mind that this retired incumbent was one of the chief protagonists for the creation of this new office. But my conviction to this effect is not predicated just on hearsay. It is also based on a conversation, which the Judge had with me and my wife, Ruth, while we attended the annual 1976 or 1977 judicial conference of the Court of Appeals of the Third Judicial Circuit at Tamiment, Pennsylvania. He spoke passionately of the urgent need to have the office created, fretted that he did not know—could not see—why the Legislature was taking so much time in doing so and implied that when the office was created, he would surely be the appointee and so the first incumbent of the new office.

Since the bill, if enacted, would be administered by the new Chief Judge, Verne A. Hodge, and he had considerable influence with both the Governor and the Legislature, somehow he was drawn into the action of deciding as to what would be the precise final provisions of the Act. The result was that the bill was radically reworked to make it possible for not just a limited few of the former judges or Judge Hoffman alone but all former judges of the Courts of the Virgin Islands to be appointed as senior sitting judges.

But another provision of the bill would probably drive the last nail in the coffin as far as Judge Hoffman being an appointee—not to mention the first or worse, the only appointee to fill the new office—was concerned. This provision would, in the end, work so that not only would he not be the only appointee or the first appointee but almost certainly would never receive an appointment to this office. This provision was to the effect that the Chief Judge of the Territorial Court only was given the authority to make appointments to the office. And it appeared that Judge Hodge and Judge Hoffman had a long, sorry volatile history of incompatibility, having its roots in the years that then-Attorney Hodge practiced law before Judge Hoffman.

I really cannot be entirely sure of this, but it appears to me that as soon as Judge Hodge was drawn into the undertaking for the creation and filling of the office, he became clearly aware of the type of person(s) he believed would work best with him to bring to fruition and fulfillment the legislative intent underlying the creation of the office. And to him, Judge Hoffman just was not such a person. So the incredible occurred. The bill became law all right, but the person who apparently built a mansion for himself lost it, and a person who was entirely unaware of the whole affair was invested as the first appointee to the new office.

Senior Sitting Judge Alphonso A. Christian I

I was that person. And I must say that Judge Hodge and his associate judges and I have had a most pleasant and fruitful relationship, which has redounded to the benefit of all the people of the Islands whom we serve.

As the Scriptures put it, "The rejected stone became the chief stone of the corner."

L to R Chief Judge Verne A. Hodge, Senior Sitting Judge
Alphonso A. Christian I, Judge Eileen Petersen

CHAPTER XIX

A Final Perspective

As a practicing member of the Roman Catholic Church, I remember well being taught by our Redemptorist Fathers and the Belgian Sisters under—whose direct tutelage I was especially privileged to be for ten consecutive years—that it is a cardinal doctrine of the Church that its members should not believe in the concept of predestination. To me, this doctrine of the Church is no expedient, timeworn, ancient teaching that generations of Roman Catholic preachers and teachers repeat from one generation to the next. On the contrary, it is a most vital, practical, useful, and reasonable ageless teaching.

If the rule were otherwise, why should anyone strive to make the correct spiritual and religious choices? Why should anyone bother to set worthy goals for self-advancement, for the uplift of society as a whole? Would there be any point in struggling for the good, let alone the best—for excellence—if one's destiny is forecast in cement, is predestined by some force over which he has no control?

But while I do not believe in predestination, I do believe that God does have a special place for each of His creatures, which can be achieved with fitting effort, when the right choices predicated on right doctrine are made in life—that for each man, struggle and perseverance in the right can yield special, albeit different, positive beneficial achievements. To paraphrase, I do believe that each man is given his own special gifts, which he can identify and develop by putting his shoulders to the wheel and making the proper and required amount of effort. So that each of us should not look covetously (or worse, enviously) at the other man's special gifts (developed or undeveloped) but rather look carefully at ourselves to identify those special gifts with which Providence has endowed us and then work unflaggingly to develop these—our own special gifts—to their highest potential.

Consider the two clear alternatives and their intrinsic value or lack of value to one's self and to one's society. Where one takes the route of serious searching, objective self-analysis to identify and does identify his special gifts, and then proceeds to do his very best to develop those gifts—allowing no obstacle to stop him—the inevitable result is that person's very own maximum special contributions to himself and his society. Indeed a creative, positive, valuable contribution to the upliftment of himself and his society.

Daughter, Cora presenting a portrait of Judge Christian to him painted by famous local artist, Dove, at ceremony becoming Honorary Member of the Lion's Club for Outstanding Service

It is indeed agonizing to even contemplate the result where one opts for the opposite course, believing in predestination—what will be will be. There he stands, worrying to death about the fact that others are doing so well in their special areas, although they are not his but theirs. And so the petulance, fretting, fuming, whining, self-pitying, envying, hating continue ad infinitum, indeed ad nauseam. So instead of making, growing, and prospering by the positive choice, utter waste and destruction result from opting for what is clearly the negative, clearly foolish, choice in the course of conduct taken in one's brief lifetime, so brief indeed that there is not too much time to correct major blunders in choosing one's philosophy and course in life.

And while I do not believe in predestination, I not only believe that each man is endowed with special gifts to be identified and developed for his individual and the collective good but I also deeply believe that Providence somehow provides certain very special opportunities to each man to develop his or her special gifts. These special opportunities could be the parents we have, the teachers we get, the gift of our particular religious faith, positions we happen to achieve, and the places we happen to find ourselves in—even certain illnesses, sufferings, crosses, disappointments we happen to have to endure, which may really and truly turn out to be blessings in disguise, if you will. In most of these vicissitudes of life, we may have had no direct hand or choice.

Who among us chose our parents, our first religious faith, early teachers, or was able to choose exactly the first job we wanted or received? Or who could predict the illnesses and other crosses he would have to bear?

Would it not be wise, then, to subscribe to the principle to always beat the iron of opportunity while it is hot—realizing that opportunity (especially great ones), as a rule, does not strike more than once? And then without permitting ourselves to be quagmired in believing in the concept of predestination after we have carefully determined our special gifts and made the best of them (assisted by those very special aids, which are bestowed on each of us), should we not freely decide (realistically put our finger on) the things we cannot change and wisely decide to accept them (with the complete satisfaction that we have done the best with those special, unique gifts and attributes, which we received)?

This chapter is dedicated especially to the young of our community, for it is they who are making their first choices as to the courses they will pursue in life and who I therefore believe can benefit most from the thoughts expressed in this chapter. If they can manage to use what I call a final perspective as their first perspective, perhaps they will be able to plan and lead more rewarding and self-fulfilling lives.

Marcus, grandson- entrepreneur; Nesha, granddaughter, attorney, son-in-law, Simon, author, professor of Economics and Dean of the College of Liberal Arts and Social Studies daughter, Cora, physician, author and administrator son, Alphonso II, attorney, daughter, Barbara, author and professor of African American Studies at University of California Berkeley Alphonso, Dad, & Ruth. Mom

Renewal of wedding vows of Ruth and Alphonso after 50 years of marriage at Sts. Peter and Paul Cathedral by Bishop Sean Patrick O'Malley

CHAPTER XX

Conclusion

Judge Alphonso A. Christian
88 years old

Why is one motivated to write, to record, his memoirs? My primary reason is that I truly believe I had some experiences and occurrences in my life that might prove of some interest to succeeding generations, and if I at all could find the time, I was duty bound to record them for posterity, yes, especially my own direct and collateral descendants.

But there were some catalysts. First, I made the mistake of letting my children know that I was seriously thinking of undertaking this work. And all of them—especially the academicians, Barbara and my son-in-law, Simon—not only began the cajoling, encouraging, and at times, the prodding but they would not let me off the hook. Almost always, when we met, I was greeted in part by the question, "How are the memoirs coming along? We are so eager to start reading how things went with you as you coursed your way through life and your life's work." And the academicians tried to flatter me by laying great emphasis on what they claimed to be a fact—that there were so few such works to be found in our local schools, universities, and public libraries.

Nor were my friends who heard of the idea much different. Their interest was whetted by their knowledge of my personality, particularly my notorious penchant to be brutally frank in expressing things exactly as I saw and knew them. As our deceased councilman of a prior era—old rock hind, the venerable, most interesting, and witty Weymouth Rhymer—used to put it, "With the bark off." If their friend Alphonso wrote it, it was likely to be just what happened and written with little or no superficial veneer. Maybe, just maybe, they might learn a fact or two and get a laugh or two as a bonus.

Attorneys Desmond Maynard, Francis Jackson, Marshall A. Bell, and others I do not remember have done their fair share of prodding. I hope they will now let me off the hook—in fact, give me a well-deserved respite.

But the greatest pressure group of all were my employees, who helped type the initial drafts. They seemed more interested in reading and typing the rough drafts of these memoirs than doing their regular work, or any other office work for that matter. Was their deep interest generated most by the historical aspect of the work—by the fact that they found a tinge, albeit so small, of melee in the work? Or is it by their interest in what they could learn from it, adopt from it, and profit from it in their own lives? Or perhaps a number or all these reasons? I will never really know. But my secretaries just loved typing these manuscripts chapter by chapter. And invariably, the question would be, "When will the next chapter be ready?"

So I have to admit the fact that I had encouragement aplenty to write these memoirs. I must truly thank all the members of my family, my friends, all my secretaries, who did so much and contributed so much to bringing this task to complete fruition. All who read and benefit in any way or to any degree from this work, like me, are deeply in their debt.

May I finally conclude by thanking the Giver of all good gifts for what I consider to be a very rewarding life. It is his gift, his stewardship to me. I preserve it to the best of my ability while I am privileged to use it and then I rededicate it to him to be passed on and reentrusted to whomever he wills.

BOOK REVIEW OF MY MEMOIRS: AN AUTOBIOGRAPHY

This colorful memoir of a profoundly influential leader is required reading for anyone interested in a first-person account of the history, social, cultural, and political of the Virgin Islands. The read is charming stylistically, full of facts, and illustrative stories. Invidious discrimination between persons rich and poor and light and dark-skinned pervades this account of the judge's life. Most interesting is how the development of political power begins to turn that class structure on its head. The judge, with other giants of Virgin Islands history, saw the ways and means to power and formed the first organized political party—The Progressive Guide. The guide changed the course of island history. Patriarch Ralph Paiwonsky and the upstart politician Earle B. Ottley established a political machine. Business leaders and their role in history are described in fascinating detail through the eyes of one learning how to achieve power. Christian's decision to become a lawyer in order to overcome the limitations of his position was inevitable as is his ascension to the bench. Tales of the Judge's demeanor and encounters on and off the bench are legendary. The reader will enjoy, empathize with, and laugh out loud at this account of the trials, tribulations, adventures, and achievements of this legend of Virgins Islands history.

—Adriane J Dudley, Esq

Judge Alphonso A. Christian's *My Memoirs: An Autobiography* is not just the story of a remarkable Virgin Islander's life, it provides a candid window on the political, social, cultural, judicial, and economic history of the Virgin Islands of the United States of America during the challenging, dynamic, and turbulent 20th century.

The author in this frank, straightforward, informative, and readable autobiography does not mince words in telling of the successes, challenges, and shortcomings of Virgin Islands society during his lifetime. He was born in a large family in the town of Frederiksted in the western end of St. Croix in 1916 during the very last months and days of Danish Colonial rule. Christian, through the recollections, reflections, and the narratives of his parents and grandparents, gives the readers a glimpse of life in the Danish West Indies, especially St. Croix—including the personal feelings of various segments of the population at the time.

In the sphere of the political evolution of the Territory, Christian played an active role. He was an early and ardent member of the Progressive Guide of the Virgin Islands. This organization was founded in St. Thomas in 1937 as the first political party in the Virgin Islands to be established in accordance with the Organic Act of June 22, 1936, the then de facto constitution of the Territory.

In *My Memoirs: An Autobiography*, Christian tells of the birth of the organization and of its visionary founders—Carlos Downing, Omar Brown, and Henry V. Richards. He outlines the evolution of the party and its contributions in improving the economic, social, and political lives of the people of the Virgin Islands, especially of the working class.

Nonetheless, Christian does not fail to disclose the shortcomings and failures of the party, including the infightings and rivalry among its members, especially the leaders. This led to the downfall of the organization in the early 1950s.

In the areas of social and economic development, despite the notable improvements made by the Naval Administration (1917-1931) and the early years of civilian governance (1931-1954), Judge Christian vividly reveals the sordid conditions under which the majority of Virgin Islanders lived as late as the mid-1950s.

"Health conditions were...quite bad. The infant mortality rate was about 50%. The buildings used for hospitals and clinics were poorly designed, the special needs woefully inadequate, the technical personnel just not provided."

In *My Memoirs: An Autobiography*, Judge Christian, as a professional lawyer and jurist, as one expects, gives an account of his ups and downs as a judge as well as his career as a barrister in general. He is candid in his assessment of the judicial system revealing its strengths as well as its weaknesses. He does not hesitate to discuss his own grievances relating to what he considered unfair treatment of him by fellow judges and lawyers.

As a devout lifelong member of the Roman Catholic faith and the recipient of a solid Catholic education, Christian made sure that *My Memoirs: An Autobiography* is replete with references to Almighty God the Creator and references of his own deep religious feelings. In it he portrays, often in vivid and deep details, the devoted service and deep influence of the strict but caring Belgian nuns and inspiring Redemptorist priests who educated generations of students in the parochial schools of the Virgin Islands, St Croix in particular.

Despite its broad and invaluable insights in various aspects of the political, social, cultural, and economic life of the people of the Virgin Islands during his remarkable life, *My Memoirs: An Autobiography* is in essence the tale to a large degree of a self-educated, self-made, ambitious, talented Virgin Islander, who in the face of many challenges and obstacles rose from the underclass in a mostly impoverished Caribbean Territory to a well-lived life fraught with worthy contributions to his homeland and beyond.

Every student, teacher, scholar, or lover of Virgin Islands and Caribbean history and culture in general would want to have a copy of *My Memoirs: An Autobiography* in his or her library and a second copy to give as a gift to a like-minded friend or colleague.

—Charles W. Turnbull, Ph.D.
Governor of the U.S. Virgin Islands 1999-2007

This writer has had the distinction of being invited by the editor of this volume to share some observations on the life of the late Honorable Judge Alphonso Christian. The several cultural projects I have been involved with which focused on the Virgin Islands and the Caribbean were probably reason for this invitation. Moreover, sometime earlier, Cora L.E. Christian, MD, MPH had passed on to me the journal kept by her father and asked for my comments.

(It took a while to fulfill her request, but a year or so later I sent her my report.)

I was as excited at that time about the prospect that Judge Christian's journal might be published as I am today on learning it is in the process of publication.

My primary interest in Alphonso's account of his life from childhood in Fredrikstead on St. Croix to retirement from the judgeship on St. Thomas, Virgin Islands has turned on his straightforward, no holds barred account of the obstacle course he valiantly confronted and navigated through in achieving his career and professional goals.

Briefly, Alphonso Christian presents us with a crash course as he narrates his life from earliest childhood in rural St. Croix. Where his lifelong lessons and precepts on class, Caste and Industry were passed on by a wise grandfather. On through the gauntlet of social and racial barriers, he would have to confront on urbanizing and bustling St. Thomas, in his function in the work place, and in his personal quest for decent housing (all of this through his meteoric rise in the Justice system, to his retirement at the summit, as Senior Sitting Judge in the Virgin Islands.)

Judge Christian has a lot to share with us—including, importantly, the younger and future Virgin Islanders—and all who might read his journal, on each of the following topics (but not only on those):

Stepparenting, the value of Education, the give-and take between Idealism and Industry, the probity aspect of Probate and how it ramifies critically with the underclass, Religious Conviction, and the balance between what might be predestined and what is distributed through Providence.

When faced with acts of bad will, including malice and treachery, he suggests a clean break (where possible and appropriate), and "move on!" He faced his share of them—and moved on!

Finally, below, I quote partially and amend from my earlier review the following might provide the current reader a fair retrospective into my approach to the judge's journal

> *The minutiae of societal mores related by Christian are, in this writer's view, of immense importance for the cultural researcher who would wish to consider him/herself knowledgeable, even tangentially, on the question: When are Virgin Islanders to be viewed as bona fide West Indians and when not. Or, for that matter, as Afro-Americans and not!*

For the above reasons and more, the Memoires of Judge Alphonso have earned my recommendation of "Required Reading" for all who might embark on a course on Virgin Islands and Caribbean Culture and History and Recommended Reading for political activists and reformists in our territory and region.

On the subject of Balancing Opportunity and Enfranchisement, the memoirs should be a handbook!

—Gilbert A. Sprauve Ph.D
(Emeritus Professor of Modern Languages, UVI)

ABOUT THE AUTHOR

 Cora L. E. Christian's dad, Judge Alphonso A. Christian I, is the author.

She, as he stated, was the catalyst for this reflective account of his life up to 1991. He lived an additional twenty-four (24) years and passed away one week before his ninetieth (90th) birthday. Although she was the catalyst and, some would say, harassed him to write a historical yet personal account about his life experiences, he captured the complexity of his own story with the national and international events on the world stage of the times. This cannot be denied. Also, what cannot be denied is that her sister Barbara, famous in her own right, was the first female African American full professor at the University of California-Berkeley. She received the Berkeley Citation, the highest award given to any University of California-Berkley professor. Barbara was instrumental in starting the Black Women's Novelist Movement in the United States of America, teaching and encouraging Black women, like Toni Morrison and Alice Walker. Barbara egged him on to continue. Simon—her husband of almost half a century, who similarly had humble beginnings but rose to a full professor of economics and dean at his alma mater and an ambassador from his native land— egged her dad on too.

Most importantly, his friends, colleagues, and employees— especially the secretaries who painstakingly typed the manuscript for her dad's handwriting that would never have earned high grades for penmanship from the nuns—enjoyed this extracurricular work so much that they, too, pushed him to write more. Cora, too, had to persevere to retype the manuscript from the old typewritten format with syllabized words to a computer. Even if the manuscript was sent to the publisher, she missed a few words despite many, many days of retyping.

Cora is his last child. He described in his memoirs "that my [his] Black children would be given nothing less than the best any White child received in upbringing—from before conception, during gestation, after birth, in childhood, adolescence, and even after the formal educational years were spent, if necessary, to become established in their chosen fields for their life's work. No child, White or Black, would have a better chance to survive and compete if only the child had what it takes and would let me help."

All his children have been rewarded, for that resolution was a promise fulfilled. They attended schools like Notre Dame, Columbia, Harvard, Johns Hopkins, Jefferson Medical College, and Howard University. Cora's brother—Alphonso II, named after their dad, a Notre Dame and Harvard Law graduate—was a senior partner of Chief Justice John Roberts at Hogan and Hartson Law Firm. Personally, her preparation academically was an undergraduate degree from Marquette (they had to attend a Jesuit undergraduate school), a medical degree from Jefferson Medical College, a public health degree from the best public health school in the world (Johns Hopkins University), a residency in Family Medicine from Howard University (one of the best HBCUs)—and all this by age twenty-five (25). At age twenty-three (23), she became the first native female to become a physician. This allowed her, at a young age, to contribute from one of the United States of America's tiniest, most easterly geographic locations and 85 percent minority population—the United States Virgin Islands—to chair an HBCU Foundation for ten years; to be a delegate to the AMA and AAFP, the two most influential medical organizations in the USA; to be sergeant at arms at the AAFP's Congress of Delegates for many years; to be on the national board of AARP, the largest volunteer organization of forty million

(40,000,000); to jobs where she was the only woman of color in a man's industry at the largest oil refinery in the Western Hemisphere; to publishing in medical journals and contributing to several chapters of books; and to the faith organization, SGI, that practices what her dad preached, although she is a Buddhist and he was Catholic. But still, Cora knew that she had an obligation to function in all that she did to ensure that to everyone she cared for, every organization she belonged to, and her two children—Nesha and Marcus, her greatest treasures—she would give 100 percent at every moment. He taught them not only with his words but with his example.